The Message of the Old Testament

The Message of the Old Testament

The Old Testament Speaks, Abridged Edition

Previous title,
The Old Testament Speaks, Third Edition.

Samuel J. Schultz

1817

Harper & Row, Publishers, San Francisco

Cambridge, Hagerstown, New York, Philadelphia, Washington
London, Mexico City, São Paulo, Singapore, Sydney

THE MESSAGE OF THE OLD TESTAMENT. Copyright © 1986 by Samuel J. Schultz. All rights reserved. Printed in the United States of America. No part of this book may be used or reproduced in any manner whatsoever without written permission except in the case of brief quotations embodied in critical articles and reviews. For information address Harper & Row, Publishers, Inc., 10 East 53rd Street, New York, NY 10022. Published simultaneously in Canada by Fitzhenry & Whiteside, Limited, Toronto.

This work is an abridgement of a work previously published under the title *The Old Testament Speaks*, Third Edition.

FIRST EDITION

Library of Congress Cataloging-in-Publication Data

Schultz, Samuel J.
  The message of the Old Testament.

  Includes indexes.
  1. Bible. O.T.—History of Biblical events.
I. Schultz, Samuel J. Old Testament speaks. II. Title.
BS1197.S332 1986   221.9′5   86-383
ISBN 0-06-067135-1

86 87 88 89 90 MPC 10 9 8 7 6 5 4 3 2 1

CONTENTS

	Introduction	1
1.	The Period of Beginnings	5
2.	The Patriarchal Age	10
3.	Emancipation of Israel	20
4.	Preparation for Nationhood	28
5.	Occupation of Canaan	36
6.	The Kingdom of Israel	47
7.	The Kingdom Divided	65
8.	The Northern Kingdom	75
9.	The Southern Kingdom	87
10.	Return from Babylon	107
11.	Interpretation of Life	125
12.	Isaiah and His Message	139
13.	Exile and Restoration Hopes	154
14.	Minor Prophets—The Twelve	165
	Appendix	175
	Scripture Index	189
	Subject Index	191

ILLUSTRATIONS

Figures

1. The Patriarchal World ca. 1800 B.C. (map) — 177
2. The Route of the Exodus ca. 1400 B.C. (map) — 178
3. The Annual Calendar (chart) — 179
4. The Conquest of Canaan ca. 1400–1300 B.C. (map) — 180
5. The Era of Transition ca. 1100 B.C. (map) — 181
6. The Davidic Empire ca. 1000 B.C. (map) — 182
7. Kings and Prophets—Divided Kingdom, 931–586 (chart) — 183
8. The Divided Kingdom ca. 860 B.C. (map) — 184
9. The Assyrian Empire ca. 700 B.C. (map) — 185
10. The Babylonian Empire ca. 600 B.C. (map) — 186
11. Exilic Times (chart) — 187

INTRODUCTION

The Bible lives today. The God who spoke and acted in times past confronts this generation with the written word as preserved in the Old Testament. Our knowledge of ancient cultures in which this record originated has been greatly increased through archaeological discoveries and the advancing frontiers of biblical scholarship. *The Old Testament Speaks,* published in 1960, was designed to introduce the liberal arts student and lay reader to the history and literature of the Old Testament, offering an outline of the entire Old Testament in the light of contemporary knowledge. This volume offers an abridgment of the third edition (1980) of *The Old Testament Speaks.*

In my graduate studies I was exposed to a wide range of Old Testament interpretation under the late Dr. Robert H. Pfeiffer at Harvard University as well as Drs. Allan A. MacRae and R. Laird Harris at Faith Theological Seminary. To these men I am indebted for a critical understanding of the basic problems confronting the Old Testament scholar. It is not without an awareness of the conflict in contemporary religious thought regarding the authority of the Scirptures that the biblical view of revelation and authority is projected as the basis for a proper understanding of the Old Testament. Since this analysis is based on the literary form of the Old Testament as it has been transmitted to us, questions of authorship are only occasionally noted and pertinent facts of literary criticism are mentioned in passing.

Charts are provided to aid the reader in a chronological integration of Old Testament developments. Maps are designed to aid the reader to understand geographical factors as they affected contemporary history.

Interest in the Old Testament is universal. Millions of people turn to its pages to trace the beginnings of Judaism, Christianity, or Islam. Countless others are attracted by its literary excellence. Scholars diligently study the Old Testament for the archaeological, historical, geographical, and linguistic contribution it makes toward a better understanding of Near East culture preceding the Christian Era.

In world literature the place of the Old Testament is unique. No book—ancient or modern—has had such worldwide appeal, been transmitted with such exacting care, and been accorded such extensive distribution. Acclaimed by statesman and servitor, learned and illiterate, rich and poor, the Old Testament comes to us as a living book. Poignantly it speaks to each generation.

According to internal evidence, the Old Testament was written during a period of approximately a thousand years (ca. 1400–400 B.C.) by at least thirty different authors. The authorship of a number of books is unknown. The original language of most of the Old Testament was Hebrew, a branch of the great family of Semitic languages, which includes Phoenician, Assyrian, Babylonian, Arabic, and other tongues. Down to exilic times Hebrew continued as the spoken language of Palestine. In the course of time Aramaic became the lingua franca of the Fertile Crescent, so that parts of Ezra (4:8–6:18; 7:12–26), Jeremiah (10:11), and Daniel (2:4–7:28) were written in this language.

Until A.D. 1488, when the first Hebrew Bible appeared in print in Soncino, Italy, every copy was handwritten. Before the discovery of the Dead Sea Scrolls in 1947, the earliest Hebrew manuscript extant dated back to about A.D. 900. In these scrolls of the Qumran community, which was dispersed shortly before the destruction of Jerusalem in A.D. 70, every Old Testament book except Esther is represented. Evidence from these recent discoveries has confirmed the viewpoint that the Hebrew text preserved by the Masoretes was handed down without serious changes from the first century B.C.

Does the Old Testament come to us simply as a narrative of secular history or culture? Does it have value merely as the national literature of the Jews? The Old Testament itself purports to be more than the historical record of the Jewish nation. To Jews and Christians alike, it is the sacred history that discloses God's revelation of himself in mighty acts and the spoken word. The dialogue between God and humanity begins with Adam and continues throughout the Old Testament through the prophets. Thus the Old Testament is a historical record of the divine–human relationship expressed in deed and word unfolding God's plan for the future of humanity.

Throughout the fortunes and misfortunes of Israel, God, the creator of the universe as well as of human beings, ordered the course of his chosen people in the international arena of ancient cultures. God is not only the God of Israel but the supreme ruler who controls the affairs of all nations. Consequently the Old Testament does record natural events, but also interwoven throughout this history are the supernatural activities of God. This distinctive feature of the Old Testament—the disclosure of God in historical events and messages—raises it above the level of secular literature and history. Only as sacred history can the Old Testament be understood in its full significance. Recognition that both the natural and the supernatural are vital factors throughout the Bible is indispensable to a full-orbed comprehension of its contents.

Unique as sacred history, the Old Testament claims distinction as Holy Writ. Such it was to the Jews, to whom these writings were entrusted, as well as to the Christians (Rom. 3:2). Coming through the natural medium of human authors, the final written product was divinely approved. Surely the Spirit of God employed the attention, the investigation, the memory, the imagination, the logic—all the faculties of the writers of the Old Testament. In contrast to mechanical means, God's guidance was manifested through free exercise of the author's historical, literary, and theological capabilities. The written record as received by Jews and Christians constituted a divine-human product inerrant in its original writing. As such it contained the truth for the entire human race.

Such was the attitude of Jesus Christ and the apostles. Jesus, the

God-Man, accepted the authority of the entire body of literature known as the Old Testament and freely used these Scriptures as the basis of appeal in his teaching (See John 10:34-35; Matt. 22:29, 43-45; Luke 16:17; 24:25). So did the apostles in the early years of the Christian church (2 Tim. 3:16; 2 Pet. 1:20-21). Recorded by human beings under divine guidance, the Old Testament was accepted as entirely reliable and trustworthy.

In our day it is just as essential to let the Old Testament constitute the ultimate authority, as it did in New Testament times for Jews and Christians. As a reasonably reliable record—allowing for errors of transmission that need careful consideration by the scientific use of correct principles of textual criticism—the Old Testament speaks authoritatively in the language of the layman of two or more millennia ago. What it enunciates it declares truthfully—whether it employs figurative language or literal, whether it deals with ethics or with the natural world of science. The words of the biblical writers —properly interpreted in their total context and in their natural sense according to the usage of their day—teach the truth without error. As such, let the Old Testament speak to the reader.

This volume offers an abridged survey of the entire Old Testament. As archaeology, history, and other fields of study are related to the content of the Old Testament, may they be the means of gaining a better understanding of the Bible's message. But only to the extent that the reader allows the Bible to speak for itself will this book accomplish its purpose.

S. J. S.

Lexington, Massachusetts
May 1985

Chapter 1

THE PERIOD OF BEGINNINGS

The Old Testament provides an answer to our inquiry into the past. Delineated in the first eleven chapters of Genesis are the essential facts regarding the creation of this universe and of human beings, extending into the past beyond that which has been definitely established or corroborated by historical investigation. Basic to the entire revelation unfolded in the Old and New Testaments, these chapters can be accepted unequivocally and with reasonable assurance as the "first" (and the only authentic) account of God's creation of the universe.

How shall we interpret this account of the beginning of human beings and their world? Is it mythology, allegory, a contradictory combination of documents, or a single person's idea of the origin of things? Other biblical writers recognize it as a straightforward narration of God's activity in creating the earth, the heavens, and human beings. But the modern reader must guard against reading into the narrative, interpreting it in scientific terms, or assuming it to be a storehouse of information bearing upon recently developed ologies. In interpreting this section of the Bible—or any other text, for that matter—it is important to accept it on its own terms. Without question the author made normal use of symbols, allegory, figures of speech, poetry, and/or other literary devices. To the author, it apparently constituted a sensible, unified record of the beginning of all things as made known by God through human and divine means.

The time covered by this period of beginnings is nowhere indicated in the Scriptures. Whereas the terminal point—the time of

6 / THE MESSAGE OF THE OLD TESTAMENT

Abraham—is related to the first half of the second millennium, the other events of this era cannot be dated with exactness. Attempts to interpret the genealogical references as a complete and exact chronology do not seem reasonable in the light of secular history. Although the narrative generally is in chronological sequence, the author of Genesis by no means suggests a date for creation.

Most important in these eleven chapters of Genesis is the fact that God is the creator of all things, with human beings unique among all creatures. Consequently this material provides the foundation for the delineation of the creator–creature relationship in subsequent chapters.

The Account of Creation—Genesis 1:1–2:25

"In the beginning" introduces the preparation of the universe for the creation of human beings. Whether this dateless date refers to God's original creation or to God's initial act in getting the world ready for human beings is a matter of interpretation. Sequence and progression mark the era of creation and organization. In a period designated as six days, order prevailed in the universe relative to the earth.

The focal point of this account is the creation of Adam and his relationship to God and the world about him (1:26–2:25). Like other creatures Adam was formed from the ground (2:7; cf. 2:19) and animated by the "breath of life" (2:7; cf. 1:30; 6:15; 7:22). Uniquely distinguished from all other creatures, Adam was created in "the image of God" (1:27). He had the capacity to understand God's command to name the animals, to work and care for the "Garden of Eden." Having created Adam for this purpose, God commanded him to rule over all creatures and, under divine blessing, "fill the earth and subdue it."

The distinction between human beings and animals is further apparent in the fact that Adam found no satisfactory companionship until God created Eve as his helpmeet. Entrusted with the full enjoyment of all things God had so abundantly provided, Adam and

Eve had only one restriction—not to eat of the tree of the knowledge of good and evil.

The Fall and Its Consequences—Genesis 3:1–6:10

Most crucial in the human relationship with God is the drastic change that was precipitated by disobedience (3:1–24). As the most tragic development in the history of the human race, it is a recurrent theme in the Bible.

Confronted with a serpent who spoke, Eve began to doubt God's prohibition and deliberately disobeyed. Adam in turn yielded to Eve's persuasion. Immediately they were conscious of their deception by the serpent and their disobedience to God. With aprons of fig leaves they tried to conceal their shame. Face to face with the Lord God, all parties involved in this transgression were solemnly judged. The serpent was cursed above all animals (3:14). Enmity was to be the perpetual relationship between the seed of the serpent, who represented more than the particular reptile present, and the seed of the woman. In regard to Adam and Eve, God preceded judgment with mercy by assuring ultimate victory through the woman's seed (3:15). But woman was consigned to sorrow in childbearing, and man was subjected to the consequences of a cursed earth. God provided skins for their clothing, which involved the killing of animals in behalf of sinful human beings. Conscious of the knowledge of good and evil, Adam and Eve were immediately expelled from the Garden of Eden lest they also partake of the tree of life and live forever. Banished from the habitat of bliss, they faced the consequences of the curse, with the promise of eventual relief through the seed of the woman to mitigate their fate.

The attitude of their sons Cain and Abel toward God is reflected in the quality of their offerings. Fruit as well as animals were subsequently prescribed as acceptable offerings (see Lev. 1–5). Cain merely offered "some" of the fruit, while Abel offered the "fat portions," or the best of the firstborn, of his flock. Cain's disrespect for God persists when he ignores the divine warning and kills his brother Abel.

Following the loss of Abel and their disappointment in Cain, now a murderer, the first parents expressed a new hope in the birth of Seth. Noah, born generations later as a descendant of Seth, lived when the godlessness of civilization reached a crisis. Corruption, wickedness, and violence increased to the extent that God regretted having created humanity and planned to withdraw his spirit from them. A period of one hundred twenty years of warning preceded the pending judgment of the human race. Only Noah found favor in the eyes of the Lord. Blameless and righteous, he maintained an acceptable relationship with God.

The Flood and Humanity's New Beginning—Genesis 6:11–11:32

Noah and his family were divinely secured in the ark for approximately one year while a flood came as a judgment upon all. Whether the Flood was local or worldwide is of secondary importance to the fact that the deluge extended far enough to accomplish God's purpose in destroying all humankind.

Civilization after the Flood began with sacrificial offerings. In response God made a covenant with Noah and his descendants. The rainbow in the sky became the perpetual sign of God's everlasting covenant. Blessing Noah, God commissioned him to populate and possess the whole earth. Properly slaughtered animals, as well as vegetation, were ordained for food. Human beings, however, were held strictly accountable to God—in whose image they had been created—for the shedding of blood.

Turning to agrarian pursuit, Noah planted a vineyard. His indulgence in intoxicating wine resulted in a breach of modesty to which Ham, and probably his son Canaan, responded with disrespect. This incident became the occasion for paternal utterances of curse and blessing by Noah (9:20–28). Noah's verdict was prophetic in scope. He anticipated the sinful attitude of Ham reflected in the line of Canaan, one of Ham's four sons. Centuries later the wicked Canaanites were subjected to severe judgment when their land was occupied by the Israelites.

Being a racial and linguistic unit, the human race remained in one location for an indefinite period (11:1-9). On the plain of Shinar they undertook a tremendous building project. The construction of the Tower of Babel represented pride in human achievement as well as defiance of God's commission to populate the earth. God, who had continually taken an interest in human beings since their creation, could not ignore them now. Apparently the Tower of Babel was not completely destroyed, but God terminated the endeavor by causing linguistic confusion. This resulted in the willing dispersion of the human race.

A genealogical listing of Noah's descendants, representing a long era, merely suggests areas to which various families migrated. After this genealogical framework using ten generations, the record finally focuses upon Terah, who migrated from Ur to Haran. The climax is the introduction of Abram (later known as Abraham), who embodies the beginning of a chosen nation—the nation of Israel—which occupies the center of attention throughout the rest of the Old Testament.

Chapter 2

THE PATRIARCHAL AGE

The world of the patriarchs is geographically identified as the Fertile Crescent. Stretching from the Persian Gulf along the Tigris and Euphrates basin and then southwestward through Canaan to the fertile Nile Valley, this area was the cradle of prehistoric civilizations. The beginnings of history coincide with the development of writing in Egypt and Mesopotamia (ca. 3500–3000 B.C.). When the patriarchs come on the scene in the second millennium B.C. the Mesopotamian and Egyptian cultures already boasted of a millenniel past. With Canaan as the geographic center for the beginnings of a new nation, the Genesis account is interrelated with the milieu of the two early civilizations, beginning with Abraham in Mesopotamia and ending with Joseph in Egypt (Gen. 12–50).

The Sumerians, a non-Semitic people who controlled the lower Euphrates area known as Sumer (ca. 2800–2400 B.C.), gave us the first literature in Asia. For the cuneiform world, Sumerian became the classical language, and it flourished in writing throughout Babylonian and Assyrian cultures until about the first century B.C. The Sumerians were second to none in antiquity in the field of metallurgy, as well as in the crafts of goldsmith and gem cutter. They used chariots for javelin throwers in battle and the phalanx, which was so effectively used by Alexander the Great many centuries later. Their basic principles of construction are utilized by modern architects. Their power extended from Ur on the lower Euphrates as far west as the Mediterranean.

The Akkadians, with Akkad north of Ur as their capital, replaced the Sumerians as the dominating kingdom and extended into Asia Minor for about two centuries. They adopted the culture of the Sumerians, using their writing for the Semitic Babylonian tongue. Tablets uncovered at Nuzi indicate that this Old Akkadian period was a time of prosperity in which the installment plan was used commercially throughout the empire. A clay map among the records is the oldest known. Akkadian power reached its height under Naram-Sin, whose stela of victory can be seen in the Louvre in Paris.

The Akkadians were conquered by the Gutians from the north, who occupied Babylonia for about a century after which they gave way to the aggressive Sumerian rulers of Erech and Ur. Sumerian culture was revived under Ur Nammu, founder of the Third Dynasty of Ur, where he erected a great ziggurat. There Nannar, the moon-god, and his consort, Nin-Gal, the moon-goddess, were worshiped during the golden age of Ur.

After a century of supremacy this Neo-Sumerian dynasty collapsed, and the land of Sumer reverted to the old system of city-states. This afforded the Amorites, or western Semites, an opportunity to gain ascendancy. Under Zimri-Lim, whose capital was Mari, they extended their influence (ca. 1750 B.C.) from the middle Euphrates into Canaan.

About 1700 B.C. Hammurabi, who had developed the small village of Babylon into a great commercial center, was able to conquer Mari, extending his domination over the upper Euphrates and Tigris areas, including the kingdom of Shamshi-Adad I, whose capital was Ashur. Marduk, the chief god of Babylon, gained prominent recognition in his empire. Most significant of Hammurabi's achievements was his code of law, discovered in 1901 at Susa, where it had been taken by the Elamites when his kingdom fell. Since old Sumerian customs were incorporated in these laws, it is likely that they represent the culture that prevailed in Mesopotamia in patriarchal times.

When Abraham came to Egypt, this land could boast of a culture more than a thousand years old. The beginning of Egyptian history is usually traced to King Menes (ca. 3000 B.C.), who united two kingdoms—one in the Delta and another in the Nile Valley. The first era of international commerce in historical times flourished under the first two dynasties. Thebes in Upper Egypt was their capital.

The classical age of Egyptian civilization, known as the Old Kingdom period (ca. 2700–2200 B.C.) and comprising Dynasties III–VI, witnessed a number of notable achievements. Huge pyramids, the wonder of the centuries to follow, provide ample testimony to the advanced culture of these early rulers. The Step Pyramid at Saqqara, the earliest large structure made of stone, was built as a royal mausoleum by Imhotep, an architect who also gained renown as a priest, author of proverbs, and magician. The Great Pyramid at Giza towered 481 feet from a thirteen-acre base. The gigantic Sphinx near it has never been equaled. "Pyramid Texts" inscribed on walls of chambers and halls indicate that the Egyptians in their sun worship anticipated a hereafter. The proverbs of Ptahhotep, vizier under a pharaoh of the Fifth Dynasty, are noteworthy for their practical advice.

After a two-century decline, the Middle Kingdom (ca. 2000–1780 B.C.) emerged under the powerful, centralized government of the Twelfth Dynasty with its capital near Memphis. Palace schools trained officials in reading and writing, making it possible for average individuals to enter government service by means of education, training, and special ability. Classical literature flourished. "The Tale of Sinuhe" is the finest example of literature from ancient Egypt designed to entertain. "The Song of the Harper," another masterpiece from the Middle Kingdom, enjoins one to enjoy the pleasures of life.

When this kingdom declined, the Hyksos intruders, who probably came from Asia Minor, occupied Egypt. They overpowered the Egyptians by means of horse-drawn chariotry and the composite bow, both of which were unknown to Egyptian troops, and established Avaris in the Delta as their capital. Shortly after 1600 B.C. the Theban rulers became powerful enough to expel this foreign power and to establish the Eighteenth Dynasty, introducing the New Kingdom.

Canaan was strategically located between these two great centers that cradled the earliest civilizations, and it served as a natural bridge linking Egypt and Mesopotamia. Extending in length 150 miles from Beersheba north to Dan, Canaan (or Palestine) has an area of six thousand square miles between the Mediterranean Sea and the Jordan River. The average width is forty miles, with a maximum of fifty-four miles from Gaza to the Dead Sea, narrowing to twenty-eight miles at the Sea of Galilee. With the addition of four thousand square miles east of Jordan (Transjordan), this land comprises about ten thousand square miles, slightly larger than the state of Vermont.

With the migration of Abraham from Ur to Haran and then to Canaan, this land becomes the focal point in the historical and geographical developments of biblical times.

The Biblical Account—Genesis 12-50

Current consensus of scholarship accords the patriarchs a place in the history of the Fertile Crescent in the first half of the second millennium B.C. The assertion (by J. Wellhausen in 1878) that the biblical account consists of nothing more than fabricated legends has been replaced by a general respect for the historical quality of these chapters in Genesis. Largely responsible for this revolutionary change was the discovery and publication of the Nuzi tablets, as well as other archaeological information that has come to light since 1925. Although no concrete evidence is available to identify from external sources any specific names or events with those mentioned in the Genesis account, it is easy to recognize that the cultural milieu is the same for both. The sole evidence for the existence of Abraham comes from the Hebrew narrative, but many Old Testament scholars now recognize him for his place in the beginnings of Hebrew history.

The date for Abraham cannot be fixed with absolute certainty. Based on certain chronological notations given in the Scriptures, the entrance of Abraham into Canaan is calculated to have taken place in 2091 B.C. This allows 215 years for the patriarchs in Canaan, 430 years for Israelites in Egypt, and an early date for the Exodus (1447 B.C.).

More illumination of the cultural, historical, and chronological context of patriarchal times may come from the excavations at Tell Mardikh, which has been identified as Ebla, about forty-four miles south of Aleppo, Syria. In 1974, a royal palace was uncovered with an estimated fifteen to twenty thousand tablets written in Sumerian and Eblaic, including the earliest vocabularies yet known. A variety of administrative records, religious literature, business and commercial accounts, and personal names and places will provide further knowledge about this ancient city and its extended contacts.

Ebla appears to have been a very important center in northern Syria, where four or five kings from one dynasty ruled during the Early Bronze era (ca. 2400–2200 B.C.) With an advanced culture and a well-defined language, this kingdom had extended influence in the Fertile Crescent from the highlands of Mesopotamia to Sinai in the south until Ebla was destroyed by Naram-Sin of Akkad. From these vast resources in ancient Ebla, it may be possible to correlate the Genesis accounts with this culture preceding patriarchal times.

Abraham—Genesis 12:1–25:18

In Ur and Haran, where Abraham lived before he migrated to Canaan, the moon-god Nannar was worshiped as the principal deity. In obedience to God's command Abraham left the highly civilized city of Haran and, accompanied by Lot, his nephew, traveled some four hundred miles to the land of Canaan, where he stopped at Shechem (about thirty miles north of Jerusalem). In addition to an excursion to Egypt, which was necessitated by famine, Abraham halted at such well-known places as Bethel, Hebron, Gerar, and Beersheba. Sodom and Gomorrah, the cities of the plain to which Lot migrated, were directly east of the South Country, or Negeb, where Abraham settled.

Abraham was a man of considerable wealth and prestige. Although the evaluation of his possessions is summed up in a simple statement —"all the possessions they had accumulated and the people they had acquired in Haran" (12:5)—it is likely that his wealth was represented by a large caravan when he migrated to Palestine. A force of 318 servants used subsequently to deliver Lot (14:14) and a caravan of ten camels (24:10) signify but a token of Abraham's material resources. Servants were added by purchase, gift, and birth (16:1; 17:23, 27; 20:14). Palestinian chieftains recognized Abraham as a prince, with whom they made alliances and concluded treaties (14:13; 21:22; 23:6).

From the standpoint of social institutions, the Genesis record of Abraham is a fascinating study. Abraham's plan to make Eliezer heir of his possessions, since he did not have a son (15:2), reflects the Nuzi laws that provided that a childless couple could adopt anyone they chose as a son. Such a son would have full legal rights and would be rewarded with the parents' inheritance in return for constant care for them and their proper burial at death. Marital customs from Nuzi, as well as the code of Hammurabi, provided that, if a man's wife had no children, the son of a handmaid could be recognized as the legal heir. Hagar's relationship to Abraham and Sarah is typical of the customs that prevailed in Mesopotamia. Abraham's concern for Hagar's welfare may also be explained by the fact that legally a handmaid who bore a son could not be sold into slavery.

A devotional study of Abraham also can be rewarding. God's promise to bless him became a reality in his personal experience as well as in subsequent times. His name was made "great" not only as the father of the Israelites and Mohammedans but also as the great example of faith for Christian believers in the New Testament writings of Romans, Galatians, Hebrews, and James. The promise to bless all the families of the earth unfolds into a worldwide scope when Matthew opens his account of the life of Jesus Christ by stating that he is the "son of Abraham."

The covenant plays an important role in Abraham's experience. Note the successive revelations of God after the initial promise to which Abraham responded in obedience. As God enlarged this promise, Abraham exercised faith that was reckoned to him as righteousness (15:6). The land was specifically pledged to the descendants of Abraham. With the promise of the son, circumcision was made the sign of the covenant. This covenant promise was finally sealed in

Abraham's act of obedience when he demonstrated his willingness to sacrifice his only son, Isaac.

The religion of Abraham is a vital theme in this account. Leaving a culture and a family that served other gods (Josh. 24:2), Abraham became repeatedly known for building "an altar to the Lord." After he had rescued Lot and the king of Sodom, he refused a reward, acknowledging that he was wholly devoted to God, the "maker of heaven and earth." The intimate communion and fellowship that existed between God and Abraham is beautifully portrayed in chapter 18, where he intercedes for Sodom and Gomorrah. Later he is identified as a "friend of God" (Isa. 41:8; James 2:23).

Isaac and Jacob—Genesis 25:19–36:43

The character of Isaac as portrayed in Genesis is somewhat obscured by the eventful lives of both his father and his son. He inherited his father's wealth and engaged in agriculture, living in Gerar and Beersheba.

Controversial in character, Isaac's son Jacob emerged as the inheritor of the covenant. In line with Nuzi customs he negotiated with Esau to secure inheritance rights. His bargaining ability is readily apparent in his acquisition of firstborn rights for the meager price of a dish of lentils. Esau's unrealistic sense of true values may have been due to temporary fatigue and exhaustion from a fruitless hunting expedition. In addition, Jacob gained the deathbed blessing through trickery and deception instigated by his mother, Rebekah. The significance of this acquisition is better understood by comparison with contemporary laws that made such oral blessings legally binding. Noteworthy, however, is the fact that the biblical account emphasizes the place of leadership above material blessing.

Fearing Jacob's probable marriage to Hittite women as well as Esau's revenge, Rebekah engineers a plan to send her favorite son to Padan-aram. There Jacob negotiates a contract with Laban, Rebekah's brother, for the marriage of his daughters, Rachel and Leah. As he gained great wealth Jacob sensed serious tension in his relationship with Laban. Encouraged by God to return to the land of his fathers, Jacob gathered his possessions and departed unexpectedly when Laban was away on a sheep-shearing mission. After seven days Laban overtook him and searched for his household teraphim, which Rachel successfully hid. According to Nuzi law, a son-in-law who possessed the household idols could claim the family inheritance in court—an advantage Rachel tried to obtain for Jacob. But Laban nullified any such benefit by a covenant with Jacob before they parted.

Continuing toward Canaan, Jacob anticipated the dreaded meeting with Esau. Overwhelmed with fear he turned to God in prayer for deliverance. During the loneliness of the night he had a divine encounter in which his name was changed from "Jacob" to "Israel." After making peace with his brother, Jacob moved on into Canaan. At Bethel he removed idolatry from his household, built an altar, and received the covenantal assurance that not only one nation but a company of nations and kings would emanate from Israel. Finally he arrived in Hebron, the home of his father, Isaac.

Joseph—Genesis 37:1–50:26

In one of the most dramatic narratives in world literature, the experiences of Joseph entwine patriarchal life with Egypt. Here we note the continuity of Mesopotamian influence, the adaptation to the Egyptian environment, and above all the controlling guidance of God in the fascinating fortunes of Joseph and his people. Joseph, the son of Rachel, was Jacob's pride and joy. To show his favoritism, Jacob garbed him with a tunic, apparently the distinctive mark of a tribal chief. His brothers, who already resented Joseph for his evil reports concerning them, were incited by this to greater hatred. The matter came to a head when Joseph related to them two dreams foretokening his exaltation. The older brothers gave vent to their feelings by getting rid of Joseph at the first opportunity.

Sent by his father to Shechem, Joseph could not find his brothers until he came to Dothan, approximately eighty miles north of Hebron. After subjecting him to ridicule and abuse, the brothers sold him to Midianite and Ishmaelite traders who subsequently disposed of him as a slave to Potiphar in Egypt. Confronted with Joseph's bloodstained coat, Jacob mourned the loss of his favorite son in the belief that he had been torn by wild beasts.

The setting for Joseph's experiences in the land of the Nile has been shown to be authentic in many details. Egyptian names and titles occur, as could be expected. Potiphar is designated as "captain of the guard" or "chief of executioners," which was used as the title for the king's bodyguard. Asenath (an Egyptian name), the daughter of a priest of On (Heliopolis), becomes the wife of Joseph. Important officials in the Egyptian court are appropriately identified as "chief cupbearer" and "chief baker." Egyptian customs are likewise reflected. Being a Semite, Joseph wore a beard, but for his appearance before Pharaoh he was shaved in conformity to Egyptian ways. The fine linen robe, the golden necklace, and the signet ring adorned Joseph in typical Egyptian fashion when he assumed administrative command under Pharaoh. *"Abrech,"* probably an Egyptian word meaning "to take note," is the order to all Egyptians upon the inauguration of Joseph. The embalmment of Jacob and the mummification of Joseph also followed the Egyptian pattern of caring for the deceased.

Parallels between the life of Joseph and Egyptian literature also are noteworthy. Joseph's transition from slave to ruler resembles the Egyptian classic "The Eloquent Peasant." The seven lean years and the seven years of plenty in Pharaoh's dreams are similar to an ancient Egyptian tradition.

Throughout these years of adversity, suffering, and success the human–divine relationship is clearly apparent. Tempted by Potiphar's wife, Joseph did not yield or sin against God. In prison Joseph frankly confessed that the interpretation of dreams belonged to God. When he appeared before Pharaoh, Joseph acknowledged that God used dreams to reveal the future. He also took God into consideration in his interpretation of history; in revealing his identity to his brothers he humbly credited God for bringing him to Egypt. Not in the least did he call them to account for selling him into slavery. After Jacob's death, Joseph reassured them once more that he would not seek revenge. God had ordered the events of history for the good of all.

Joseph's magnification of God through many vicissitudes was rewarded by his own elevation. In Potiphar's house he was so trustworthy and efficient that he was promoted to overseer. Thrown into prison on false charges, Joseph was soon entrusted with supervisory responsibilities, which he used wisely to help his fellow prisoners. Two years after the butler was restored to the palace, he remembered Joseph, who then was suddenly brought before Pharaoh to interpret the king's dreams. Made chief administrator, he not only guided Egypt through the years of plenty and famine but was instrumental in allotting the land of Goshen to the Israelites when they migrated to Egypt.

Jacob's blessings form a fitting conclusion to the patriarchal age in the Genesis account. On his deathbed he uttered his last will and testament. Even though he was in Egypt, this blessing reflects the custom of the Mesopotamian homeland, where oral pronouncements were recognized as binding when contested in court. In keeping with the divine promises made to the patriarchs, Jacob's blessing, given in poetic form, had prophetic significance.

For additional study help see *Figure 1* in the Appendix.

Chapter 3

EMANCIPATION OF ISRAEL

Centuries pass in silence from the death of Joseph to the dawn of national consciousness under Moses. Sacred history, however, takes on new and exciting dimensions with the unique transition of the Israelites from the pharaonic clutches of slavery to the status of an independent nation as God's chosen people. In less than a lifetime they undergo a miraculous deliverance from the mightiest emperor of the day, receive a divine revelation that makes them conscious of being God's covenant people, and have imparted to them a code of laws in preparation for occupying the land of patriarchal promise. It is not surprising that this remarkable experience was retold and relived annually in the observance of the Passover. Repeatedly the prophets and psalmists acclaim Israel's deliverance from Egypt as the most significant miracle in their history.

So meaningful was this emancipation and so vital was this involvement between God and Israel for coming generations that four fifths of the Pentateuch, or more than one sixth of the entire Old Testament, is devoted to this short period in Israel's history. Beyond the years of Egyptian oppression, which received brief consideration in the introductory chapters, the events of these four books—Exodus, Leviticus, Numbers, and Deuteronomy—are confined to less than five decades. A summary of the material is provided in the following outline:

From Egypt to Mount Sinai	Exodus 1–18
Encampment at Mount Sinai	Exodus 19–Numbers 10

Wilderness wanderings	Numbers 10–21
Encampment before Canaan	Numbers 22–Deuteronomy 34

Contemporary Events

There is no disagreement among scholars, who accept the historicity of Israel's bondage in Egypt, that the Exodus occurred during the New Kingdom era. Since the closing chapters of Genesis already account for Israel's migration to Goshen, the contemporary events in Egypt are of primary importance.

With the expulsion of the Hyksos rulers, the New Kingdom (ca. 1546–1085 B.C.) began with the Eighteenth Dynasty. In this dynasty, Thutmose III (ca. 1504–1450) established the absolute power of Egypt by asserting himself as the greatest military leader in Egyptian history. In eighteen campaigns he extended the control of his kingdom to the Euphrates, marching his armies through Palestine or sailing the Mediterranean Sea to the Phoenician coast. As a military man and empire builder he is often compared with Alexander the Great and Napoleon. Since these campaigns were executed in summer, he usually promoted large-scale building projects during the winter, beautifying and enlarging the great temple at Karnak, which had been erected to Amun during the Middle Kingdom. Obelisks erected by him may be seen today in London, New York, the Vatican, and Istanbul.

Amenhotep IV, better known as Akhenaton (ca. 1379–1362 B.C.), effected a revolution in religion. He championed the worship of Aton, who was represented by the solar disk. Building a temple at Thebes to his new god while he was still coregent with his father, he proclaimed himself the first priest of Aton. He selected Amarna, midway between Thebes and Memphis, as his capital and established the worship of Aton as the state religion. The archives of Amarna, discovered in 1887, bear witness to the fact that he was so devoted to his religion that he was oblivious to appeals for aid from various parts of the kingdom. When he died this new capital was abandoned. His son-in-law, Tutenkhamon, secured his throne by renouncing

Aton and restoring the former Theban god. The tomb of Tutenkhamon, discovered in 1922, provided abundant evidence of his devotion to Amun.

Noteworthy in the Nineteenth Dynasty is Ramses II (ca. 1304–1237 B.C.). In his attempt to reconquer Syria he eventually signed a peace treaty—the earliest nonaggression pact between nations known today—with the Hittite king. During the next two dynasties weaker rulers struggled to retain their kingdom. As the central power decreased, the local priesthood of Amun gained enough strength to establish the Twenty-first Dynasty about 1085 B.C. Egypt never regained her position as a world power.

Religion in Egypt

Egypt was a land of many gods. With local deities as the basis of religion, Egyptian gods became numerous. Nature gods were commonly represented by animals and birds. Eventually cosmic divinities, which were personified in the forces of nature, were elevated above the local gods and were theoretically considered as national or universal deities. They were so plentiful that they came to be grouped in families of triads and enneads.

Temples likewise were numerous throughout Egypt. With the provision of a home or temple for each god came the priesthood, the offerings, the festivals, rites, and ceremonies for worship. In return for these accommodations the people looked to their gods as benefactors. Fertility of land and animals, victory or defeat, the flooding of the Nile Valley, in fact, every factor affecting welfare in this life, was ascribed to some god.

The national prominence accorded any one god was closely related to politics. The falcon god, Horus, rose from a local to a state deity when King Menes united Lower and Upper Egypt at the dawn of Egyptian history. When the Fifth Dynasty patronized the sun-god of Heliopolis, Re became the head of the Egyptian pantheon. The nearest approximation to a national god in Egypt was in the recognition given to Amun during the Middle and New Kingdoms. The magnificent temples at Karnak and Luxor, near Thebes, still bear witness to the royal patronage of this god. In the Eighteenth Dynasty the Amun cult with its Theban priesthood became so strong that the pharaonic challenge to its power was successfully squelched upon Akhenaton's death. Despite the prominence of the national gods, at no time were they worshiped exclusively by the Egyptian populace. To an Egyptian peasant the local god was all-important.

Egyptians believed in life after death. A blameless record here on earth entitled one to immortality. This accounts for the royal burials represented by the pyramids and other tombs, in which adequate provision, such as food, drink, and the luxuries of life, was made for the hereafter. In early times servants were even slain and placed beside their master's body. Like Osiris, the divine symbol of immortality, the deceased Egyptian anticipated trial before a tribunal of the underworld with the hope of being morally fit for the bliss of eternal life.

Extreme tolerance in the Egyptian religion accounts for the endless addition and recognition of so many gods. None were ever eliminated. The modern student finds it difficult to make a logical analysis of the multitudinous unrelated elements of this religion, but it is doubtful that any native Egyptian did. Confusion results from any attempt to correlate the host of deities with their respective cults and rituals. Neither can the host of myths and beliefs be rationalized.

The Date of the Exodus

That Israel left the land of bondage during the latter half of the second millennium B.C. hardly remains subject to question. Since no references or incidents in the Book of Exodus can be definitely correlated with Egyptian history, absolute dating bears further investigation. Suggested dates range from 1450 B.C. to 1200 B.C.

The biblical record provides limited data for establishing a definite date for the time of Israel's Egyptian bondage. Only one chronological reference specifically links the Solomonic era—which has well-established dates—with the Exodus. The assumption that the 480 years noted in 1 Kings 6:1 provide a basis for exact dating yields a date for the Exodus near 1450 B.C. Although other references and the account of intervening developments point to a long time between the deliverance from Egypt and the kingdom era in Israel, none of the biblical passages involved warrant precise dating.

More numerous are the biblical notations approximating the period preceding the Exodus. Even though problems of interpretation are yet unsolved, they convey the impression that the Israelites spent several centuries in Egypt. Genealogical references may suggest a comparatively short period of time between Joseph and Moses, but the use of a genealogy as a basis for time approximation is still subject to question. Genealogies often have long gaps that make them unsuitable for fixing chronology. The increase of the Israelites from seventy to a great multitude that threatened Egyptian rule likewise favors the lapse of centuries for Israel's residence in the land of the Nile.

Biblical considerations bespeak longer chronologies before and after the Exodus. On this basis it is reasonable to consider about 1450 B.C. as a date for the Exodus and allow for the migration of Jacob and his sons in the era of Hyksos supremacy in Egypt.

The Biblical Account—Exodus 1:1–19:2

Israel's dramatic deliverance from Egyptian bondage is vividly portrayed in Exodus 1:1–19:2. Beginning with a brief reference to Joseph and the adverse fortunes of Israel, the historic developments center around Moses, culminating in the emancipation of Israel.

Under Joseph the Israelites had been granted the most fertile area in the Nile Delta. After the expulsion of the Hyksos, the Egyptian rulers in the course of time promoted policies oppressing the Israelites. In such perilous times Moses was born.

Adopted by Pharaoh's daughter, Moses was educated in all the wisdom of the Egypt (Acts 7:22), the foremost center of civilization. Royal heirs from Syria and other lands, who were brought to these educational facilities at the Egyptian court, may have been classmates of Moses, exposing him to the culture and languages of Mesopotamia.

Moses' valiant attempt to help his people ended in failure. Fearing the vengeance of Pharaoh, he fled into the land of Midian, where he spent the next forty years. Received favorably into the home of Reuel (Jethro), a priest of Midian, in the course of time Moses married Reuel's daughter Zipporah and settled down to a shepherd's life in the Midian wilderness. There Moses undoubtedly acquired a thorough knowledge of the vast desert territory through which he led the Israelites years later.

The call of Moses is indeed significant in the light of his background and training. Not without reason was he reluctant to ask for Israel's release, knowing from experience that he would have to contend with the authority of Pharaoh. God assured Moses of divine aid and provided three miracles to accredit him before the Israelites —the rod that became a serpent, the leprous hand, and water turning to blood. This provided a reasonable basis for the Israelites to believe that Moses had been commissioned by the God of the patriarchs. Having been assured that Aaron would be his spokesman, Moses complied with God's call and returned to Egypt.

The Contest with Pharaoh

During the New Kingdom period the power of Pharaoh was unsurpassed among contemporary nations. His domain at times extended as far as the Euphrates. Moses' appearance at the royal court demanding the release of his people Israel presented a challenge to Pharaoh's power.

The plagues, coming during a relatively short period, demonstrate the power of Israel's God not only to Pharaoh and the Egyptians but also to the Israelites. Pharaoh's attitude from the very beginning is that of defiance, expressed in the question, "Who is the Lord that I should obey him and let Israel go?" When confronted with the opportunity to comply with God's will, Pharaoh resists, hardening his heart in the course of these developments. The purpose of the plagues —clearly stated in Exodus 9:16—is to show Pharaoh the power of God on behalf of Israel. The ruler of Egypt is challenged by supernatural might.

How extensively the Egyptians were affected by the plagues is not fully stated. The last plague was designed to bring judgment on all the gods of Egypt. The inability of Pharaoh and his people to counteract these plagues must have demonstrated to the Egyptians the superior power of Israel's God compared with the helplessness of the gods they worshiped. This caused some Egyptians to acknowledge the God of Israel (Exod. 9:20).

Israel likewise became conscious of divine intervention. Having been in bondage for several generations, the Israelites had not witnessed a demonstration of God's power in their day. Each succeeding plague brought a greater manifestation of the supernatural, so that with the death of the firstborn the Israelites realized that they were being delivered by One who is omnipotent.

The plagues are best explained as a manifestation of God's power through natural phenomena. Neither the natural nor the supernatural element should be excluded. The first nine plagues are distinctly associated with natural phenomena in the Nile Valley, beginning with an unusually high flood in July or August. The effects of such an excessive inundation would have lasted into October or November, leaving an abundance of dead fish to plague the Egyptians. Swarms of frogs dying en masse, lice or gnats in abundance, swarms of insects or flies plaguing the people, severe pestilence on livestock, fine dust causing boils to erupt in open sores on humans as well as animals, a heavy hail destroying barley and flax in February, swarms of locusts in March to consume new growth, and an extraordinary dust storm, making the air so thick and dark that it obscured thelight of the sun for three days—these were the plagues that came in sequence and confronted Pharaoh with the God of the Israelites. Intensity, timing, and duration were miraculously evident in portraying the power of God in contrast to the impotence of the many gods of Egypt.

The tenth and final plague was wholly supernatural. The clearest credentials of God's authority and power were apparent in his precise and full control of the death of only the firstborn in each family in Egypt. For the Israelites this event marked the hour of their deliverance. Carefully following divine instructions, each Israelite household killed a lamb or goat. The blood was applied to the doorframes, and the meat was roasted, providing a meal in preparation for leaving Egypt. The blood was the visible sign to exclude each family from the death of their oldest son. So significant was the application of the blood—the first interpretation given in Scripture of the meaning of blood in an offering—that this observance was designated as the "Lord's Passover." This was to be observed annually by the Israelites, reminding them that the Exodus was the greatest miraculous event in Old Testament times.

Israel's journey to Canaan via the Sinai peninsula was divinely ordered. No doubt the direct route—a well-traveled road used for military and commercial purposes—would have brought them to the promised land in a fortnight. Leaving Egypt the Israelites witnessed the miraculous presence and power of God in a pillar of cloud by day and a pillar of fire by night for their guidance and protection. When the Israelites saw God's display of his mighty acts in their emancipation from Egypt, "the people feared the Lord and put their trust in him and in Moses his servant" (Exod. 14:31). With the Red Sea and the Egyptians behind them, the Israelites moved southward, divinely led by a luminous cloud. With the miraculous provision of water, manna, and quail, they were reminded of God's daily care. In less than three months they arrived at Mount Sinai, where they encamped for approximately one year.

For additional study help see *Figures 2* and *3* in the Appendix.

Chapter 4

PREPARATION FOR NATIONHOOD

Israel's encampment at Mount Sinai was purposeful. In less than a year's time God's covenant people became a nation. The covenant expanded in the Decalogue and laws for holy living, construction of the tabernacle, organization of the priesthood, the institution of offerings, observances of feasts and seasons, and the organization of the camp—these enabled Israel to serve God effectively (Exodus 19:1–Num. 10:10).

The religion of Israel was a revealed religion. For centuries the Israelites had known that God had made a covenant with Abraham, Isaac, and Jacob, but they had not been experientially conscious of his power and manifestation on their behalf. God was mindful of this covenant in delivering Israel out of Egyptian bondage and slavery (Exodus 6:2–9). It was here at Mount Sinai that God revealed himself to Israel.

Love and obedience—not law—is the key to the relationship established between God and Israel in this covenant (Exodus 20:1–24:8). The focal point in this God–human relationship was that God would continue "showing his love to thousands who love me and keep my commandments" (Exodus 20:6). The Ten Commandments are basic stipulations concisely expressing God's will for his people in maintaining this relationship. The first four express the responsibility individual Israelites have to God, who has redeemed them from slavery. Love and loyalty are essential. The six commandments that follow regulate behavior toward other members of society. Love and respect for others issue out of God's concern for them. God's love and holiness are to be reflected in the life of the God-revering person in his or her relationship with other people. Out of the vertical relationship with God issues a proper horizontal relation toward one's neighbor.

Monotheism is the distinctive feature of the Decalogue, in contrast to polytheism in Egypt and in Canaan, where many gods were worshiped. The plagues had been directed against Egyptian gods. Israel was to be distinct and unique as God's own people, characterized by a singular devotion to God and God alone. Not even an image or likeness of God was permissible; idolatry was one of the worst offenses in the religion of Israel.

Expansion of the moral laws and additional regulations for holy living were designed to guide the Israelites in their conduct as God's holy people (Exodus 20–24; Lev. 11–26). Simple obedience to these moral, civil, and ceremonial laws would distinguish them from the surrounding nations.

These laws for Israel can better be understood in the light of the contemporary cultures in Egypt and Canaan. Marriage of brother and sister, which was common in Egypt, was forbidden. Regulations regarding motherhood and childbirth not only reminded them that human beings are sinful creatures but stood in contrast to sex perversion, prostitution, and child sacrifice associated with the religious rites and ceremonies of the Canaanites. Pure food laws and restrictions concerning the slaughter of animals were designed to keep the Israelites from conforming to some of the Egyptian customs associated with idolatrous rituals. It was fitting that the Israelites, having vivid memories of slavery, should be instructed to leave gleanings for the poor at harvest time, provide for the helpless, honor the aged, and constantly render righteous judgment in all their relationships. As more knowledge becomes available concerning the contemporary religious milieu of Egypt and Canaan, it is likely that many of the restrictions for the Israelites will seem more reasonable to the modern mind.

The moral laws were permanent, but many of the civil and ceremonial laws were temporary in nature. The law limiting the slaughter of animals for food to the central sanctuary was abrogated when Israel entered Canaan (cf. Lev. 17 and Deut. 12:20–24).

Up to this time the altar had been the place of sacrifice and worship. At Sinai Moses built an altar, with twelve pillars representing the twelve tribes of Israel, on which the young men of Israel offered sacrifices for the ratification of the covenant (Exodus 24:4 ff.). Then God instructed the Israelites to "make a sanctuary for me, and I will dwell among them" (Exodus 25:8). In contrast to the many temples in Egypt, the Israelites had only one sanctuary, or tabernacle.

This tabernacle (forty-five feet long and fifteen feet wide) was divided into two parts. The forepart contained three pieces of furniture: the table for bread on the right side, the lampstand on the left side, and beyond them the altar for the burning of fragrant incense. The holy of holies (fifteen feet square) contained only the ark of the covenant, the most sacred object in the religion of Israel. A court with a perimeter of about 450 feet enclosed the tabernacle. In the eastern half, known as the worshiper's square, stood the altar of burnt offering, where the Israelites brought their offerings. Beyond it, before the entrance into the tabernacle, stood the bronze basin, or laver, where the priests washed their hands and their feet in preparation for officiating at the altar of sacrifice or in the tabernacle.

For orderly ministry and effective worship, Aaron was designated to serve as high priest for Israel. With Moses officiating, Aaron and his sons were ordained and consecrated for the priestly ministry in Israel after the tabernacle was completed (Lev. 8:1–9:24; see also Exod. 40). The firstborn in every family belonged to God by virtue of having escaped death in Egypt at the time of the Exodus. The Levites were chosen as substitutes for the oldest son in each family to assist the priests in their ministration (Num. 3:5–13; 8:17). In this way the entire nation was represented in the priestly ministry.

Offerings were a vital part of Israel's maintaining a right relationship with God. With the dedication of the tabernacle and the inauguration of the priesthood, the bringing of offerings became a part of Israel's daily worship as a nation. Through the sacrifice of the Passover lamb (Exodus 12:1–28) the Israelites had become God's redeemed and holy people as they responded in faith and obedience (Exod. 4:31; 14:31). To maintain this relationship with God as his holy people the Israelites were instructed to bring worship sacrifices and offerings (Lev. 1:1-7:38).

The burnt offering, the most common sacrifice, was offered morning and evening each day for the entire nation. Voluntarily each Israelite could offer his offering to renew his fellowship, seek renewal or forgiveness of sin, or express his praise to God. The grain offering, which did not involve animal sacrifice, represented an act of consecration and dedication with the assurance that God was pleased with the offering of the produce of his hands. The peace or fellowship offering was a sacrifice of well-being—an optional offering in which the offerer and his family shared with the priest in a festive fellowship meal. The sin or purification offering, introduced at Mount Sinai, was essential for purification and cleansing from sin. The blood of this offering was applied to the altar to make "atonement for the altar" in preparation for making an offering. On the Day of Atonement the blood was applied to the ark of the covenant. The guilt offering, in which reparation was the distinctive feature, was required of an Israelite who had violated ownership rights, human or divine.

Throughout the year the Israelites were repeatedly reminded in their pattern of living that they were God's holy people. The weekly Sabbath was to be observed as "a day of sacred assembly . . . wherever you live," (Lev. 23:3). The first recorded observance of the Sabbath occurred en route from Egypt to Sinai (Exod. 16-17). God instructed Moses, "The Israelites are to observe the Sabbath, celebrating it for the generations to come as a lasting covenant. It will be a sign between me and the Israelites forever" (Exod. 31:16-17).

The most important annual festival was the Passover. Instituted on the night of their deliverance from Egypt, this marked their beginning as an independent nation. Annually each generation was reminded of this historic event as they observed it on the fourteenth day of Nisan (April). Fifty days later they observed the Feast of Weeks (Harvest) at the end of the grain or wheat harvest. Acknowledging the goodness of God, they were instructed to "celebrate the

Feast of Weeks to the Lord your God by giving a freewill offering in proportion to the blessing that the Lord your God has given you" (Deut. 16:10). The Feast of Tabernacles marked the climax of the religious year with an eight-day celebration in the seventh month (Tishri 15–21). Celebrated at the end of the harvest season, this marked one of the most joyous seasons for the entire family and community as they rejoiced in God's abundant blessings to them (Lev. 23:23–44).

After having encamped at Mount Sinai for almost a year, the Israelites proceeded northward toward the promised land. Nearly four decades later they arrived on the eastern banks of the Jordan River. Comparatively brief is the narration of their journey and the thirty-eight years they spent in the wilderness (Num. 10:11–22:1).

The Israelites marched as an organized unit in eleven days north to Kadesh, about forty miles south of Beersheba. From there twelve spies were sent into the land of Canaan. When they returned, ten of these men declared that occupation was impossible and stirred up public sentiment for an immediate return to Egypt. Two—Joshua and Caleb—confidently asserted that with divine aid conquest was possible. The people—unwilling to believe that God who had recently delivered them from Egypt would also enable them to conquer and occupy the promised land—became an insolent mob that threatened to stone Joshua and Caleb. In desperation they even considered selecting a new leader.

God in judgment contemplated annihilation of rebellious Israel. When Moses became aware of this he made intercession and obtained pardon for his people. Nevertheless, the ten faithless spies died in a plague, and all the people aged twenty and older, excepting Joshua and Caleb, were denied entrance into Canaan. Stirred by the death of the ten spies and the verdict of a prolonged period of wilderness wanderings, they confessed their sin. That their repentance was not genuine is apparent in their rebellious attempt to enter Palestine immediately. In this they were defeated by the Amalekites and Canaanites.

An entire generation of Israelites died in the wilderness as they repeatedly rebelled, even challenging the ecclesiastical leadership of Aaron and the political authority of Moses. Insurrectionists like Korah, Dathan, and Abiram were divinely judged so that Moses and Aaron were vindicated.

En route via Elath to the Plains of Moab, Aaron died on top of Mount Hor. Eleazar was vested in his father's garments and appointed high priest in Israel. Circumventing Edom as well as Moab, the Israelites proceeded northward to the Arnon valley. When two Amorite rulers—Sihon, king of Heshbon, and Og, king of Bashan—refused Israel passage and responded with an army, the Israelites defeated them and occupied their land north of the valley of Arnon. Here on the Plains of Moab, recently taken by the Amorites, the Israelites established their camp.

The subtle designs of the Moabites on God's chosen nation were more formidable than open warfare (Num. 22:2–25:18). Overcome with fear when the Amorites were defeated, Balak, the Moabite king, devised plans for the destruction of Israel. In co-operation with the elders of Midian he engaged the prophet Balaam from Mesopotamia to curse the people encamped across the Arnon River.

Balaam refused the first invitation, being explicitly warned not to go and not to curse Israel. The fee for divination was so enticing, however, that he yielded to Balak's repeated appeal. On this mission, which was contrary to God's clearly revealed will, Balaam had the shocking experience of being audibly rebuked by his donkey. The prophet was thus impressively reminded that he was going to Moab to speak only God's message.

Balaam faithfully declared God's message four times. On three different mountains Balak and his princes prepared offerings to provide an atmosphere for cursing, but each time the prophet spoke words of blessings. Keenly disappointed, the Moabite king rebuked him and ordered him to cease. Although Balak dismissed him without a reward, Balaam offered a fourth prophecy before he left. In this he distinctly delineated Israel's future victories over Moab, Edom, and Amalek.

Balak was more successful in his next scheme against Israel. Balaam remained and offered evil counsel to Balak (Num. 31:16); the Moabites and Midianites followed his advice and seduced many Israelites into immorality and idolatry. Incurring divine wrath, the Israelite participants were subjected to a plague in which thousands died.

Subsequently Moses allotted the land east of the Jordan River, which was excellent grazing territory though outside Canaan, to the tribes of Reuben and Gad, and half of the Manasseh tribe (Num. 32:1–42). They pledged to support the rest of the tribes in the conquest of Canaan.

Aware that he would not be permitted to cross the Jordan River, Moses appealed to the new generation—none of whom were over sixty years of age except Joshua and Caleb—as delineated in the Book of Deuteronomy. This represents a renewal of the covenant established between God and Israel at Mount Sinai. The essence of the covenant lay in the relationship between God and Israel, with the operative principle being love. It was only as Israelites, individually or collectively, responded to the love initiated by God to human beings that this relationship became operative.

Against the background of the failure of the generation that died in the wilderness, Moses appealed to the Israelites to love God—love him exclusively, wholeheartedly, without reservation, "with all your heart, with all your soul, with all your strength" (Deut. 6:5). Love was not a matter of legalistic obedience to the Ten Commandments or the law as a whole. (Cf. Matt. 22:34–40; Mark 12:28–32; Luke 10:25–28.) Love was a living relationship involving a loving commitment and wholehearted devotion to God.

God's love had been extended to the Israelites beginning with Abraham, Isaac, and Jacob (4:37) and had been displayed in Israel's liberation from Egyptian bondage. This God ("I am the Lord your God who brought you out of Egypt") the Israelites were to love exclusively: "You shall have no other gods beside me" (5:6–7).

Although Moses repeats the Ten Commandments, his focal point throughout this appeal is the first commandment, which involves exclusive love and devotion toward God. Moses does not express a legalistic concern about details of sacrifice, feasts, and seasons, or the priesthood and tabernacle as delineated in Exodus, Leviticus, and Numbers. Love for God is to be expressed in the total pattern of living (10:12–13). Obedience issues out of love for God. Reverence issues out of respect for God. That Moses is emphasizing a spiritual relationship is apparent in his admonition to "circumcise your hearts . . . do not be stiff-necked" (10:16).

No area of living was beyond this relationship established in this covenant. The legislation delineated in Deuteronomy 12–26 is a mixture of religious, ceremonial, criminal, and civil laws providing guidance for the Israelites in living as God's holy people in their contemporary culture. All of life was under God's dominion. The claim that they had a love relationship with God was to be evident in their pattern of behavior as provided in these specific stipulations.

Unique in Israelite history is the appeal Moses makes to his audience on the Plains of Moab as he leads them in their renewal of the covenant. Their decision—choosing life and good or death and evil (30:15–20)—is ultimately a matter of basic importance. Providing a written copy of the law deposited with the priests for public reading every seven years, Moses turns the leadership over to Joshua. The covenant ceremony is concluded with the song of Moses, chapter 32. Anticipating the conquest and occupation of the promised land by the Israelites, Moses encourages them with his final blessing, chapter 33. Before his death he is privileged to view the land of Canaan from Mount Nebo.

Chapter 5

OCCUPATION OF CANAAN

The long-awaited day had arrived. With the death of Moses, Joshua was commissioned to lead the nation of Israel in the conquest of Palestine, centuries after it had been promised to the patriarchs. In the meantime each successive generation of the Palestinian populace had been influenced by various peoples from the Fertile Crescent as they traversed Canaan motivated by economic and military interests.

Memoirs of Canaan

In the heyday of its success the powerful Twelfth Dynasty (2000–1780 B.C.) spasmodically extended Egyptian control through Palestine as far north as the Euphrates. In subsequent decades Egypt not only declined in power but was occupied by the powerful Hyksos, who ruled from Avaris in the Delta. Shortly before 1550 B.C. the Hyksos were expelled.

The Hittite kingdom had its beginning in Asia Minor as early as the nineteenth century B.C. By 1600 B.C. their power had so increased that they extended their domain into Syria and even destroyed Babylon on the Euphrates by 1550. Within the next century the expansion of Hittite rule was halted by two rising kingdoms.

About the time that the Hyksos people were invading Egypt and Babylonia was flourishing under the First Dynasty, best exemplified by Hammurabi, the new kingdom of Mitanni emerged in the highlands of Media. These Indo-Iranian people were composed of two groups: the common class, known as Hurrians, and the nobility, or ruling class, called Aryans. Coming from the territory east of Haran, these Mitanni people continually extended their kingdom westward so that by 1500 B.C. they reached the Mediterranean Sea. The chief sport of the Aryan people was horse racing. Treatises on the subject of raising and training horses were discovered early in the present century at Bogazköy, where they had been preserved by the Hittites who conquered the Mitanni people. By 1500 B.C. the Mitanni power halted the advance of the Hittites for about a century.

The Egyptians frequently marched their armies through Canaan to challenge Mitanni might. Thutmose III defeated the Syrians at Megiddo, advanced on to Kadesh on the Orontes River, and marched his armies across the Euphrates to end the Mitanni dominion of Syria before he died.

Friction continued between Egyptian and Mitanni might during the reigns of Amenhotep II (1450–1425) and Thutmose IV (1425–1417), so that Syria vacillated in its allegiance. Subjected to pressure from the Hittites, Artatama I, king of Mitanni, made a peaceful agreement with Thutmose IV. Under terms of this policy Mitannian princesses were married to pharaohs during three successive reigns. At this time Damascus was under Egyptian administration. The Amarna letters (ca. 1400 B.C.) reflect conditions in Syria, indicating that diplomatic and fraternal relationships existed between the royal families of Mitanni and Egypt.

Hittite power soon increased and challenged this Mitanni-Egyptian control of the Fertile Crescent. Under King Shuppiluliume (ca. 1380–1346) the Hittites crossed the Euphrates as far as Washshukkanni, reducing Mitanni to a buffer state between the Hittite kingdom and the rising Assyrian empire in the Tigris Valley. This, of course, eliminated Mitanni as a political factor in Palestine. Although the Mitanni kingdom was completely absorbed by the Assyrians (ca. 1250 B.C.), the Hurrians, known as Horites in the Old Testament, were in Canaan when the Israelites entered. Possibly the Hivites were also of Mitanni origin.

Ramses II (1304–1237 B.C.) renewed Egyptian efforts to dislodge the Hittites, who were firmly entrenched in the city of Kadesh on the Orontes supported by armies from Syria, and from Carchemish, Ugarit, and other cities of Palestine. After more than two decades of fighting, Ramses II and Hattusil, the Hittite king, concluded a treaty in 1280 B.C.—a nonaggression pact outstanding in history. Copies of this famous agreement have been found in Babylon, Bogazköy, and Egypt. Although no actual boundaries are mentioned in the treaty, very likely the Amorite state formed the neutralizing influence between the Egyptians and the Hittites.

In the days of Merneptah, Aryan invaders from the north (Mitanni) destroyed the Hittite empire and weakened the Amorites, destroying Kadesh and other strongholds. Although the Hittite kingdom disintegrated, the Hittites are frequently mentioned in the old Testament. Ramses III repulsed these invaders from the north in a great battle by land and sea and once more unified Palestine under Egyptian control. After Ramses III Egyptian power declined, allowing for the infiltration of the Aramaeans into the area of Syria, which became a powerful nation about two centuries later.

The people of Canaan were not organized into strong political units. Geographical factors as well as the pressure of surrounding nations from the Fertile Crescent, who used Canaan as a buffer territory, account for the fact that the Canaanites never formed a strong, united empire. Numerous city-states controlled as much local territory as possible, with the city well fortified to resist possible enemy attack. When armies marched through Canaan, these cities often averted attack by payment of tribute. However, when people came in to occupy the land, as Israel did under Joshua, these city-states formed leagues and united in opposing the invader. This is well illustrated in the Book of Joshua.

The location of Palestine in the Fertile Crescent and the geographical configuration of the land itself often affected cultural and political developments. Upon the alluvial plain of the Tigris and Euphrates as well as in the Nile Valley, numerous petty city-kingdoms and small principalities or districts were more than once united into a great nation. This was not so easily accomplished in Syro-Palestine, since the topography was not conducive to amalgamation. As a result Canaan was in a weaker condition, since none of the city-kingdoms was equal in strength to the invading forces that came from the stronger kingdoms along the Nile and the Euphrates. At the same time Canaan, with its fertile valleys, was the coveted prize of these stronger nations. Kinglets not strong enough to withstand invaders might find it expedient momentarily to humble themselves by paying tribute to such a kingdom as Egypt. Often, however, when the invaders withdrew, the "gifts" were discontinued. Although these city-kingdoms were easily conquered, it was difficult for the victors to retain them as permanent possessions.

The religion of Canaan was polytheistic. El was considered the chief among the Canaanitic deities. Likened to a bull in a herd of cows, he was referred to by the people as "father bull" and was regarded as creator. Asherah was the wife of El. In the days of Elijah, Jezebel sponsored four hundred prophets of Asherah (1 Kings 18:19). King Manasseh placed her image in the temple (2 Kings 21:7). Chief among the seventy gods and goddesses considered offspring of El and Asherah was Hadad, more commonly known as Baal, meaning "Lord." As reigning king of the gods he controlled heaven and earth. As god of rain and storm he was responsible for vegetation and fertility. Anath, the goddess who loved war, was his sister as well as his spouse. In the ninth century Ashtoreth, or Astarte, goddess of the evening star, was worshiped as his wife. Mot, the god of death, was the chief enemy of Baal. These and many other gods introduce the catalogue of the Canaanitic pantheon.

Since the gods of the Canaanites had no moral character, it is not surprising that the morality of the people was extremely low. The brutality and immorality in the stories about these gods is far worse than anything else found in the Near East. Since this was reflected in Canaanitic society, the Canaanites in Joshua's day practiced child sacrifice, sacred prostitution, and snake worship in their rites and ceremonies associated with religion. Naturally their civilization degenerated under this demoralizing influence.

The Scriptures attest to this sordid condition by numerous prohibitions given as warnings to the Israelites. This degrading influence was already apparent in the days of Abraham, when "the sin of the Amorites had not yet reached its full measure" (Gen. 15:16; see also 19:5). After God had extended centuries of mercy to them, Moses solemnly charged his people to destroy the Canaanites—not only to punish them for their iniquity but to prevent them with their idolatrous practices from contaminating God's chosen people (Lev. 18: 24–28; 20–23; Deut. 7:1–6; 12:31; 20:17–18).

From the long-range perspective of God's eternal relationship with humanity, it was an act of mercy to terminate a culture that was becoming more sinful with each passing generation, sparing future generations divine condemnation. Jeremiah (9:23–24; Lam. 3:22), Paul (2 Cor. 1:3), and others considered the God of the Old Testament a God of love, mercy, and compassion as well as a God of justice and righteousness. Paul warned repeatedly that ultimately all non-God-fearing people would be subjected to the wrath of God. God's mercy is everlasting upon all those who revere and love him (Ps. 103:17–18; Isa. 66:1–24).

Era of Conquest

The God–Israel relationship continued through Joshua, who was trained under Moses' tutelage. In preparation for leadership Joshua had led the Israelite army in defeating Amalek (Exod. 17:8–16) and had served as a spy, gaining firsthand knowledge of existing conditions in Palestine (Num. 13–14).

The record of Joshua's activity is incomplete. No mention is made of the conquest of the Shechem area between Mount Ebal and Mount Gerizim, but it was here that Joshua assembled all Israel to listen to the reading of the law of Moses (Josh. 8:30–35). Very likely other local areas were conquered and occupied, though not mentioned in Joshua. During his leadership, which is estimated as a period of twenty-five to thirty years, the land of Canaan was possessed and occupied by the Israelites, but by no means were all the inhabitants driven out.

Joshua sent two spies to Jericho to view the land. From Rahab, who harbored them, they learned that the inhabitants of Canaan were conscious of Israel's God, who had supernaturally intervened for Israel. A miraculous passage through the Jordan River provided confirmation that God would be with them. This provided a reasonable basis for every Israelite to exercise faith in God (Josh. 3:13-17). Two twelve-stone memorials were erected—one in the Jordan and one at Gilgal—to remind coming generations of God's mighty act in Israel's passage into Canaan.

While they were encamped at Gilgal, the rite of circumcision was administered to the new generation of Israelites, painfully reminding them of the covenant and the promise that God had made to bring them into the land of Canaan (Gen. 17:1-27). There they also observed the Passover, reminding them of their deliverance from Egyptian slavery. With the fruit of the land available to them the miraculous provision of manna ceased.

To Joshua, God imparted by a theophany the consciousness that the conquest of the land was not dependent solely upon him but that he was divinely commissioned and empowered. Even though he was in charge of Israel, Joshua was but a servant and subject to the commander of the army of the Lord (3:13-15).

The miraculous conquest of Jericho was a sample victory—a convincing demonstration to the Israelites that their enemies could be overwhelmed. When the city fell, the Israelites could enter and take possession but were not allowed to appropriate any of the spoils for themselves. The things that were not destroyed—metallic objects—were placed in the treasury of the Lord. Except for Rahab and her father's household, the inhabitants of Jericho were wiped out. Unfortunately, Achan sinned by appropriating for himself an attractive garment of Babylonian origin plus some silver and gold. For this deliberate act in defiance of the command to devote all the spoils to the Lord, Achan and his family were stoned in the valley of Achor.

Joshua supervised the military strategy involved in the conquest of Ai. After the first attempt failed because of Achan's sin, the Israelites lured the enemy forces into the open so that the thirty thousand men who had been stationed beyond the city by night were able to attack Ai from the rear and set it afire. The defenders were annihilated; their king was hanged; and the site was reduced to rubble. Contrary to their previous procedure, the Israelites were to seize the livestock and other movable property and appropriate it for themselves. Although nothing is definitely stated about the conquest of Bethel, this city probably was occupied without destruction at this time. Since the king of Bethel is listed as having been killed (12:16), it is possible that the Bethelites vacated their city and joined with the Ai armies (8:17).

Following this great victory, the Israelites erected an altar on Mount Ebal, where Joshua made a copy of the law of Moses. As the Israelites listened to the public reading of the law, they were solemnly reminded of their responsibilities (8:30–35).

The citizens of Gibeon made peace with Joshua (9:1–26). Aware that God had commanded the Israelites to wipe them out (9:24), the Gibeonites shrewdly devised and executed a plan whereby they expressed their fear of Israel's God and offered to be servants of the Israelites. Although the Israelite leaders failed to seek divine guidance, the net result was a peace treaty that saved the lives of not only the Gibeonites but also the inhabitants of the cities of Kephirah, Beeroth, and Kiriath in central Canaan.

With the capitulation of the great city of Gibeon to the Israelites, the king of Jerusalem was greatly alarmed. In response to his appeal, other Amorite kings from Hebron, Jarmuth, Lachish, and Eglon formed a coalition with him to attack the city of Gibeon. Having made an alliance with Israel, the beleaguered city immediately dispatched messengers to appeal to Israel for aid. By an all-night march from Gilgal, Joshua unexpectedly appeared at Gibeon, where he defeated and routed the enemy through the Beth-horon pass (also known as the valley of Ajalon) as far as Azekah and Makkedah.

Supernatural aid in this battle resulted in a smashing victory for the Israelites. Besides the elements of surprise and panic in the enemy camp, there were hailstones, which accounted for more casualties among the Amorites than did the fighting soldiers of Israel (10:11). Furthermore, through divine intervention a long day was afforded the

Israelites, enabling them to pursue the enemy so that the Amorite league was utterly defeated. The cities of Makkedah, Libnah, Lachish, Eglon, Hebron, and Debir, with their kings, were defeated. Although the strong city-states of Gezer and Jerusalem were not conquered, they were isolated by this campaign, so that the whole southern area, from Gibeon to Kadesh-barnea and Gaza, was under the control of Israel when Joshua led his battle-hardened warriors back to the camp at Gilgal.

The conquest and occupation of northern Canaan is very briefly described. The opposition was organized and led by Jabin, king of Hazor, who had at his command a great force of chariotry. A great battle took place near the waters of Merom, with the result that the Canaanite coalition was utterly defeated by Joshua. The horses and chariots were destroyed, and the city of Hazor, located about fifteen miles north of the Sea of Galilee and five miles west of the Jordan River, was burned to the ground. There is no mention of the destruction of other cities in Galilee.

Joshua conquered the whole land of Canaan from Kadesh-barea to the valley of Lebanon, defeating thirty-one kings (11:16–12:24). On the east side of the Jordan rift, the area that previously had been conquered under Moses extended from Mount Hermon in the north to the valley of the Arnon, east of the Dead Sea.

Allotment of Canaan

Under the supervision of Joshua and the high priest Eleazar, the land was allotted to each of the tribes. Responsible for the religious services throughout the nation, the Levites were allotted forty-eight cities with adjoining grazing land for their flocks and herds. Six cities were designated as places of refuge where anyone could flee for safety from blood revenge in case of manslaughter. Shiloh was established as the religious center for Israel (18:1).

When Judges Ruled

The events recorded in the Book of Judges are closely related to the developments in Joshua's day. Since the Canaanites had not been fully dislodged, warfare continued as local areas or cities were reoccupied in the course of time.

The chronology for this period is difficult to ascertain. Israel had no king and lacked a political capital from which a judge would officiate. Rising to places of leadership as the local or national situation might demand, many of them were undoubtedly limited in influence and recognition to their local community or tribe. Some of them were military leaders who delivered the Israelites from the oppressing enemy; others were acknowledged as magistrates to whom the people looked for legal and political decisions. With neither central government nor capital, the Israelite tribes were ruled spasmodically without immediate succession when a given judge died. With some of the judges restricted to local areas, it is also reasonable to assume that several judgeships overlapped.

Certain fortified cities, such as Megiddo, Taanach, Jerusalem, and others, remained in the possession of the Canaanites, leaving Israel faced with continual difficulties. Consequently religious-political cycles (sin, sorrow, supplication, and salvation) would recur again and again (1:1–3:6). Through fraternization with the inhabitants the Israelites participated in Baal worship as they forsook their worship of God. Intermarriage led to further neglect of exclusive love for God, and sin and apostasy prevailed.

Judgment came in the form of oppression. With neither Egypt nor Mesopotamia powerful enough to dominate the Fertile Crescent during this era, the peoples from intermediate areas as well as city-states encroached upon Israel's possession of Canaan. These invaders oppressed the Israelites by taking their property and crops.

Repentance was the next part of the cycle. Conscious of their sin, the Israelites penitently turned to God. In response God raised up champions to challenge the oppressors and delivered Israel so that a period of rest followed.

Othniel from the tribe of Judah was the first judge. He was empowered by "the Spirit of the Lord" to repulse an invading force from upper Mesopotamia. Ehud, from the tribe of Benjamin, broke the power of Moab, who, with the support of the Ammonites and Amalekites, had oppressed the Israelites for eighteen years. Shamgar, in a brief notation, is credited for resisting the penetration of the Philistines into Israelite territory.

Deborah and Barak rose to leadership as they challenged the Canaanites who harassed Israel for twenty years. Encouraged by the prophetess Deborah, Barak led an army of ten thousand swordsmen, miraculously defeating Sisera, commander of the Canaanite fighting force of King Jabin, which had the advantage of nine hundred chariots. This victory was celebrated in a song expressing praise for divine aid (Judg. 5).

An angel of the Lord commissioned Gideon to challenge the Midianites, Amalekites, and other eastern peoples who invaded and camped in Israel and took livestock and crops. Following divine guidance Gideon led an alert company of three hundred men against these nomadic hordes. When the Midianites were awakened from deep sleep by Gideon's men, who blew their trumpets, smashed their jars, and shouted the battle cry "A sword for the Lord and for Gideon," they fled in confusion across the Jordan River. By faith in God Gideon delivered the Israelites (cf. Heb. 11:32). After Gideon died his son Abimelech asserted himself as king. His attempt to establish kingship in Israel was terminated when he was killed after three years.

Tola and Jair, who provided leadership as judges for twenty-three and twenty-two years, respectively, are briefly mentioned in Judges (10:1–5). Jephthah broke an eighteen-year oppression by the Ammonites. In early life he was ostracized from Gilead as the son of a harlot, but when the Gileadites needed a military leader they summoned him. Facing the enemy and empowered by "the Spirit of God" (11:29), Jephthah made a vow that "whatever comes out of the door of my house to meet me when I return in triumph from the Ammonites will be the Lord's, and I will sacrifice it as a burnt offering" (11:31). How he fulfilled this vow when his daughter met him after this victory is not delineated in detail. Very likely he dedicated her to tabernacle service, realizing that human sacrifice was not acceptable to God. Forfeiting posterity (11:37-40) was involved in this complete consecration, since she was his only child. Jephthah is also listed as a hero of faith by the author of Hebrews (11:32). The three judges that followed—Ibzan, Elon, and Abdon—are briefly noted as providing short periods of leadership in Israel (12:8-15).

Samson is the hero who resisted and challenged the power of the Philistines to the west while Jephthah defeated the Ammonite oppressors from the east (10:6). He was endowed with supernatural strength (13:25; 14:5, 19; 15:14) and remembered primarily for his military exploits. He undoubtedly could have done much more, but, ensnared by sin, he failed in his mission to deliver Israel. At best, he restrained the Philistines temporarily, so that Israel was not displaced from the promised land. He also is listed as a hero of faith (Heb. 11:32).

The closing chapters of Judges and the Book of Ruth described the conditions that existed in the days of heroic leaders such as Deborah, Gideon, and Samson. Without cross-references to the activities of any of the particular judges named in the preceding chapters, it is difficult to date these developments specifically. Rabbis associate the story of Micah and the Danite migration with the age of Othniel, but because of the lack of historical detail it is impossible to be certain of the reliability of this and similar rabbinical traditions. The most that can be done is to limit these events to "the days when the judges ruled" (Ruth 1:1). The closing statement in the Book of Judges seems to be appropriate for this entire period: "In those days Israel had no king; everyone did as he saw fit" (21:25).

For additional study help see *Figure 4* in the Appendix.

Chapter 6

THE KINGDOM OF ISRAEL

In the eleventh and tenth centuries B.C. Israel established and maintained the most powerful monarchy in its entire history. Neither before nor after did the nation have such extensive boundaries and command so much international respect. Such expansion was possible largely because no interference could come from the extremities of the Fertile Crescent during this era.

Neighboring Nations

In Egypt, after the death of Ramses III (ca. 1167 B.C.), the power of the kings gradually succumbed to the politically aggressive priestly family. By 1085 Heri-Hor, the high priest, began to rule from Karnak in Thebes while petty princes controlled Tanis. Egypt's loss of prestige is reflected by the disrespectful treatment afforded Wen-Amun in his journeys to Byblos as an Egyptian envoy (ca. 1080 B.C.). Not until the fourth year of Rehoboam (ca. 927 B.C.) was Egypt in a position to invade Palestine (1 Kings 14:25–26).

The archenemy that seriously threatened Israel's rise to power was Philistia. Settling on the maritime plain, the Philistines established five cities as their strongholds: Ashkelon, Ashdod, Ekron, Gaza, and Gath (1 Sam. 6:17). Besides their cultivation of the land and their lucrative sea trade, the Philistines held the secret of smelting iron. This was their advantage in their threat to overrun Israel in the days of Samson, Eli, Samuel, and Saul. Not only were the Israelites without smiths to make swords and spears, they were even dependent upon the Philistines to sharpen their farming implements. They were on the verge of being subjected to hopeless slavery by the Philistines. Although Saul offered resistance, it was David who broke the Philistine power after he learned the secrets of using iron and occupied Edom to gain access to natural resources.

Aram (Syria) was the threat to Israel's expansion to the north. Hadadezer, ruler of the most powerful Aramaean state, Zobah, extended his domain northward to the Euphrates (2 Sam. 8:3–9), overcoming the Hittite strongholds of Hamath and Carchemish, and southward beyond Damascus to the states of Maacah, Geshur, and Tob.

The Phoenicians, or Canaanites, occupied the seacoast to the north, concentrating on maritime interests. From Tyre and Sidon, they established their influence commercially throughout the Mediterranean world by trade and treaty. Hiram, king of Tyre, and David, king of Israel, found it mutually beneficial to maintain an attitude of friendship without military friction.

The Edomites, descendants of Esau and governed by kings before Israel's rise to monarchy (Gen. 36:31–39), were subdued by David. Placing garrisons throughout their land (2 Sam. 8:14), David gained natural resources, such as copper and iron from their mines, with which he broke the Philistine monopoly on the production of armament.

The Amalekites, also descendants of Esau (Gen. 36:12), were located westward of Edom toward the Egyptian frontier. Although Saul failed in his attempt to destroy them (1 Sam. 15), they are hardly mentioned after David's conflict with them at Ziklag. The Moabites were defeated by Saul, conquered by David, and tributary to Israel for about two centuries. The Ammonites were also defeated by Saul and later vanquished by David, never again to challenge Israel during the kingdom period.

Eli and Samuel

The times of Eli and Samuel mark the era of transition from the spasmodic and intermittent leadership of judges to the rise of an Israelite monarchy. These two men are not mentioned in the Book of Judges but are given consideration in the opening chapters of 1 Samuel (1:1–8:22) as an introduction to the narrative about Israel's first king.

The story of Eli serves as a background for the ministry of Samuel. As high priest Eli was in charge of worship and sacrifice in the tabernacle at Shiloh. It was to him that the Israelites looked for guidance and leadership in religious and civil affairs.

The religion of Israel was at an all-time low in the days of Eli. He failed to teach his own sons to revere God; they were "wicked men; they had no regard for the Lord" (1 Sam. 2:12). They took advantage of those who came to worship and profaned the sanctuary with baseness and debauchery common to Canaanite religion. As one would expect, they refused to heed their father's scathing denunciation of this behavior, while Israel continued to degenerate into increasingly corrupt religious practice. Although Eli was warned by an unnamed prophet that he honored his sons more than he honored God and that divine judgment was pending, he did not change his ways (1 Sam. 2:27–36).

Into this abhorrent atmosphere Samuel was brought in his childhood days and entrusted to Eli's care. Dedicated to God and encouraged by a godly mother, Samuel grew up in the environment of the tabernacle impervious to the godless influence of Eli's sons. Samuel, responding to God's call, became God's spokesman to warn Eli once more that judgment was imminent (1 Sam. 3:1–18).

Swiftly and suddenly these prophetic words received fulfillment. When they were fighting the Philistines, the Israelites prevailed upon the sons of Eli, Hophni and Phinehas, to bring the ark of the covenant, Israel's holiest object, to the battlefield, expecting that God would protect the object that represented his presence among them.

Such was not the case. The ark was taken by the Philistines; Eli's sons were killed; and the Israelites were routed. When Eli heard the shocking news, he collapsed and died. Very likely Shiloh was destroyed by the Philistines (cf. Jer. 7:12–24; 26:6–9). So demoralizing was this defeat for the Israelites that when Eli's daughter-in-law gave birth to a son she named him "Ichabod," exclaiming, "The glory had departed from Israel, for the ark of God has been captured" (1 Sam. 4:19–22).

Samuel's place in history is unique. Being the last of the judges, he exercised civil jurisdiction throughout the land of Israel. Moreover, he gained recognition as the greatest prophet in Israel since Mosaic times. He also officiated as the leading priest, though he was not of the lineage of Aaron, to whom the responsibilities of high priesthood belonged.

The Bible has preserved comparatively little about the actual ministry of this great leader. As Philistine oppression increased the Israelites turned to Samuel for leadership. Although he lived in Ramah, there is no indication that this became the religious or civic center of Israel. When the ark was returned, the Israelites kept it at Kirjath-jearim in the private home of Abinadab until the days of David. Samuel, in an effort to purge Canaanite cultic worship from Israel's ranks, gathered the Israelites at Mizpah for prayer, fasting, and sacrifice (1 Sam. 7:1–14). Word of the convocation leaked out to the Philistines, who thereupon took advantage of the situation to launch an assault. In the midst of the fray a severe thunderstorm struck fear into the hearts of the Philistine mercenaries, producing confusion and causing them to flee. Evidently the peals of thunder took on portentous meaning to the Philistines, for never again did they attempt to engage the Israelites in battle while Samuel was in command of the tribes.

Samuel's ministry extended from Dan in the far north to Beer-sheba in the south. Mizpah, Ramah, Gilgal, and Bethlehem are mentioned as places of sacrifice where he officiated as priest. In his prophetic ministry he wielded considerable influence over bands that gathered about him. Among these people may have been Nathan,

Gad, and other prophets active in David's time (1 Sam. 19:18-24).

Eventually the tribal leaders felt that they should bolster their resistance to Philistine aggression and, accordingly, clamored for a king. Reluctantly Samuel consented to the innovation of kingship and, under divine guidance, anointed Saul, a Benjamite, to be "leader over his inheritance," thereby indicating that kingship was a sacred trust. At a subsequent convocation at Mizpah Saul was publicly chosen and enthusiastically supported by the majority in the popular acclaim "Long live the king!" (1 Sam. 9:1–10:24). Since Israel had no capital, he returned to his native city of Gibeah in Benjamin.

The Ammonite threat to Jabesh-gilead provided opportunity for Saul to assert his leadership. In response to his national appeal the people rallied to his support, resulting in an overwhelming victory over the Ammonites. Assembling all Israel at Gilgal, Samuel publicly endorsed Saul as king. He reminded them that God had granted their request. On the basis of Israel's history he assured them of national prosperity, provided the king as well as the citizens obeyed the Mosaic law (cf. Deut. 17:14–20). This message of Samuel was divinely confirmed to the Israelites in a sudden rain—a phenomenon during wheat harvest. The people were profoundly impressed and appealed to Samuel for his continued intercession. Although the Israelites had turned to a king for leadership, the words of assurance from Samuel —the prophet who had stemmed the tide of apostasy and initiated an effective prophetic movement in his teaching ministry—made them conscious of his sincere interest in their welfare: "As for me, far be it from me that I should sin against the Lord by failing to pray for you" (1 Sam. 11:1–12:25).

Israel's First King

Saul enjoyed the enthusiastic support of his people after his initial victory over the Ammonites at Jabesh-gilead. True, not all viewed his accession with unfeigned satisfaction, but these diehards could not withstand his overwhelming popularity (1 Sam. 10:27; 11:12, 13). And yet, through deliberate disobedience, Saul soon ruined his opportunities for success. Because of suspicion and hatred his efforts were so misdirected and national strength so dissipated that his reign ended in utter failure.

As a warrior Saul led his nation in numerous military victories. At a strategic location on a hill three miles north of Jerusalem Saul fortified Gibeah to counteract the Philistine military superiority. By capitalizing on a successful attack by his son Jonathan, Saul routed the Philistines in the battle of Michmash. Among other nations defeated by Saul were the Amalekites (1 Sam. 13:1–15:9).

The initial success of Israel's first king did not, however, obscure his personal weakness. Twice he failed in his unique responsibility to acknowledge the prophet who represented God. Impatiently awaiting Samuel's arrival at Gilgal, Saul officiated at the sacrifice himself (1 Sam. 13:8). In his victory over the Amalekites he failed to execute the instructions of Samuel, who solemnly warned him that God is not pleased with sacrifices that are substituted for obedience. With this stinging rebuke, Samuel left King Saul to his own devices. Through disobedience, he had forfeited the kingdom.

Saul became suspicious and extremely jealous of David, who became a national hero after killing Goliath, the Philistine giant. By numerous subtle schemes, he tried to remove David, who successfully escaped every maneuver designed for his doom. In his personal relations with Saul's son Jonathan, David shared in one of the noblest friendships noted in the Old Testament. When David and Jonathan realized that the time had come for David to flee because of Saul's dastardly designs on his life, they sealed their friendship with a covenant.

David fled to the Philistines for safety. Denied refuge by Achish, king of Gath, he went to Adullam, where four hundred fellow tribesmen gathered about him. Having the care of such a large group, he in time made arrangements for some of his people to reside in Moabite country. Among the advisers associated with him was the prophet Gad.

When Saul heard that Abimelech, the priest at Nob, had furnished supplies to David en route to Philistia, he ordered his execution, along with that of eighty-five other priests. Abiathar, the son of Abimelech, escaped and joined David's fugitive band.

Before long Saul gave vent to his malicious feelings toward David by open pursuit. Several times David was seriously endangered when Saul closed in on him with his army. Several times David had the opportunity to slay the king of Israel personally, but each time he refused, acknowledging that Saul was the Lord's anointed. Although Saul was deeply moved and temporarily admitted his wrongdoing, he soon resumed open hostility. Fearing that Saul might overtake him unawares, David secured permission from Achish to reside in the Philistine city of Ziklag with his six hundred men plus women and children.

The Israelite armies retreated to Mount Gilboa in their hopeless fight against the Philistines. More than fear of the enemy troubled the king of Israel at this time. Samuel, long ago ignored by Saul, was not available for interview. Saul turned to God, but there was no answer for him by dream, by Urim, or by prophet. He was panic-stricken. In desperation he turned to spiritualistic mediums that he himself had banned in the past. Locating a woman at Endor who had a familiar spirit, Saul asked for Samuel. Whatever power this woman possessed, it is apparent in the record (1 Sam. 28:3-25) that the intervention of supernatural power in bringing up the prophet Samuel in spirit form was beyond her control. Saul was reminded once more by Samuel that through his own disobedience he had forfeited the kingdom. In his message to Saul the prophet predicted the death of the king and his three sons, as well as the defeat of Israel.

Heavy in heart and with the thought of these tragic developments awaiting him, Saul returned to camp that dismal night. In the course of the battle in the Jezreel plain the Israelite forces were routed, retreating to Mount Gilboa. During the pursuit the Philistines took the lives of the king's three sons. Saul himself was wounded by enemy archers. To avoid ruthless treatment at the hands of the enemy he fell on his sword, thus ending his own life. The Philistines won a decisive victory, gaining indisputable control of the fertile valley from the coast to the Jordan River. They also occupied many cities, from which the Israelites were forced to flee.

Tragic indeed was the termination of Saul's reign as the first king of Israel. Although God-chosen and anointed by the praying prophet Samuel, he failed to realize that obedience was essential in the sacred and unique trust afforded him by God—to be "leader over his inheritance."

Davidic Union and Expansion

David's political endeavors were marked with success. In less than a decade after Saul's death, all Israel had rallied to the support of David, who had begun his reign with only the small kingdom of Judah. Through military success and friendly overtures he soon controlled the territory from the border of Egypt and the Gulf of Aqaba to the Phoenician coast and the land of Hamath. The international respect and recognition David gained for Israel went unchallenged by foreign powers until the closing year of Solomon's reign.

The new king also distinguished himself as a religious leader. Although denied the privilege of building the Temple, he made elaborate provisions for its erection under his son Solomon. Through David's leadership the priests and Levites were extensively organized for effective participation in the religious activities of the entire nation.

The Second Book of Samuel depicts the reign of David in great detail, providing the exclusive account of immorality, crime, and rebellion in the royal family (11–20). The First Book of the Chronicles represents an independent account, focusing attention upon David as the first ruler in a continuing dynasty and tracing the genealogical background of the twelve tribes over whom David ruled (1:1–9:44).

Born in turbulent times, David was subjected to a rugged period of training in preparation for the kingship of Israel. After his anointing by Samuel and his slaying of Goliath (1 Sam. 16–17) David was requisitioned for military service and gained invaluable experience in military exploits against the Philistines. After he was forced to leave the court he led a fugitive band and ingratiated himself with the landholders and sheepmasters in southern Israel by providing protection. At the same time he negotiated successful diplomatic relations with the Philistines and Moabites while he was regarded as an outlaw of Israel.

David was in Philistine country when Saul's army was decisively defeated on Mount Gilboa. Shortly after David had rescued his wives and recovered the spoil that had been seized by Amalekite raiders, a messenger reported to him the fateful events that had taken place in Israel. Overcome by grief, David gave immortal tribute to Saul and Jonathan in one of the greatest elegies in the Old Testament. Not only had Israel lost her king, but David had lost his most intimate friend, Jonathan. When the newsbearer, an Amalekite, anticipated a reward by claiming credit for Saul's death, David ordered his execution for having touched the Lord's anointed.

After ascertaining God's approval, David returned to the land of Israel. Anointed and recognized as king by his own tribe (Judah), David began his reign at Hebron. The rest of Israel was in serious trouble when Saul's reign ended. Gibeah either was destroyed or gradually fell into ruins. Civil war and Philistine control of much of Israel's land west of the Jordan led the Israelites to respond to David's friendly and gracious gestures in bidding for their support. Without malice or vengeance David gained the recognition of all Israel during these seven and a half years in which he ruled in Hebron, while the dynasty of Saul was eliminated from political leadership (2 Sam. 1:1–4:12).

The Philistines, alarmed when David gained acceptance with the whole nation, twice attacked Israel (2 Sam. 5:17–25; 1 Chron. 14:-8–17). Twice David defeated them. Very likely this had a unifying effect.

In looking for a central, strategic location for a capital, David turned to the city of Jerusalem. The Jebusites, who had successfully resisted conquest and occupation by the Israelites, now were dislodged from this Canaanite fortress. With Israelite occupation

Jerusalem became known as the "city of David" (1 Chron. 11:7).

Successfully established as king over the twelve tribes of Israel, David reorganized the government. During his days as an outlaw he had had a following of hundreds of men. These were well organized under his command at Ziklag, and later at Hebron (1 Chron. 11:-10–12:22). These men had so distinguished themselves in military exploits that they were appointed princes and leaders. When all Israel rallied to David's support, the organization was enlarged to include the whole nation, with Jerusalem as the center (1 Chron. 12:23–40). By contracting with the Phoenicians a magnificent palace was built for David the king (2 Sam. 5:11–12).

At the same time Jerusalem became the religious center for the whole nation (1 Chron. 13:1–17:27; 2 Sam. 6:1–7:29). The ark of the covenant, which had been stored with Abinadab at Kirjath Jearim and with Obed-Edom in Gibeah, was transferred to Jerusalem. Proper worship was now restored to Israel on a national scale.

With renewed interest in Israel's religion David became desirous of building a more permanent house of worship. When he shared his plan with Nathan, the prophet, it met with immediate approval. The next night, however, God commissioned Nathan to inform the king that the building of the Temple should be postponed until David's son was established on the throne. This was divine assurance for David that his son would succeed him and that he would not be subjected to such a calamitous fate as befell King Saul. The magnitude of this promise to David, however, extends far beyond the time and scope of his son Solomon's kingdom. The seed of David included more than Solomon, since the commitment clearly stated that the Davidic throne was to be established forever. Even if iniquity and sin prevailed in David's posterity, God would temporarily judge and punish but would neither forfeit his promise nor withdraw his mercy indefinitely.

No earthly kingdom or dynasty has ever had eternal duration—such as heaven and earth. Neither did the earthly throne of David —without linking his lineage with Jesus, who is specifically identified in the New Testament as the son of David (see Matt. 1:1, etc.). This

THE KINGDOM OF ISRAEL / 57

assurance, given to David through the prophet Nathan, constitutes another link in the series of messianic promises given in Old Testament times. God was gradually unfolding the initial commitment that ultimate victory would come through the seed of the woman (Gen. 3:15). A fuller revelation of the Messiah and his eternal kingdom is given by the prophets in subsequent centuries.

Why was David denied the privilege of building the Temple? In the closing years of his reign he came to realize that he had been commissioned as a military statesman to establish the kingdom of Israel (1 Chron. 28:3; 22:8). Whereas David's reign was characterized by warfare, Solomon enjoyed a period of peace. Perhaps peace prevailed at the time David expressed his intentions to build a temple, but there is no way to ascertain in Scripture how the subsequently reported wars are related chronologically to Nathan's message. Possibly not until the end of his reign did David come to realize that the days of Solomon would be a more opportune time for building a temple.

The expansion of Davidic rule from the tribal area of Judah to a vast empire stretching from the border of Egypt to regions of the Euphrates receives scant attention in the Bible. And yet this record is of basic importance historically, since Israel was the leading nation in the Fertile Crescent at the beginning of the tenth century B.C. Fortunately archaeological excavations have yielded complementary information.

The Philistines, whom David defeated twice when he unified Israel, were in time reduced to a tributary and subservient state. The observations that the Philistines had the monopoly on iron in the days of Samuel (1 Sam. 3:19–20) and that David freely used it near the end of his reign (1 Chron. 22:3) suggest that a long chapter could have been written on the economic revolution in Israel. His period of outlawry and Philistine residence not only provided David with preparation in military leadership but undoubtedly gave him firsthand acquaintance with the formula and methods used by the Philistines to produce arms. Perhaps many of the plans for military and economic expansion were made while David was at Hebron but actually executed after Jerusalem was made the capital. The Philistines had reason to be alarmed when war-torn and defeated Israel was unified under David.

The conquest of Edom was strategically important, giving David a valuable source of iron and copper needed to break the Philistine monopoly. To protect these interests David built garrisons throughout Edom (2 Sam. 8:14). Moab and the Amalekites also became subservient, sending silver and gold to David.

To the northeast the rise of Davidic might was challenged by the Ammonite and Aramaean tribes. In the course of time David defeated this Aramaean-Ammonite alliance and gained control of their territory, reaching up to the Euphrates River. Heavy tribute in gold and bronze and extensive trade enriched Israel in an unprecedented manner. Not until the closing years of David's reign was the administration of Damascus challenged. (Cf. 2 Sam. 10:1–18; 21:15–22; 1 Chron. 19:1–20:8).

As king of the Israelite empire David did not fail to acknowledge God as the one who granted Israel military victories and material prosperity. In a psalm of thanksgiving (2 Sam. 22:1–51) David expresses his praise to the omnipotent One for deliverance from his enemies in Israel as well as from the heathen nations. This psalm is also recorded in chapter 18 of Psalms. It represents but a sample of many that he compased on various occasions during his checkered career as a shepherd boy, a servant at the royal court, an outlaw of Israel, and, finally, the architect and builder of Israel's largest empire.

Character imperfections in a member of the royal family are not minimized in the Hebrew Scriptures. A king of Israel who indulged in sin could not expect to escape the judgment of God. At the same time, David, as a truly penitent sinner, acknowledged his iniquity and thus qualified as a man who pleased God (1 Sam. 13:14).

David practiced polygamy (2 Sam. 3:2–5; 11:27). Although this is definitely forbidden in the fuller revelation of the New Testament, it was tolerated in Old Testament times because of the hardness of Israel's heart. It was also freely practiced by surrounding nations. A harem at the court was the accepted thing. Although warned in

Mosaic law against the multiplicity of wives (Deut. 17:17), David acquired many. Some of these marriages undoubtedly had political implications, such as his marriage to Michal, the daughter of Saul, and to Maacah, the daughter of Talmai, king of Geshur. Like others, David had to suffer the consequences as the crimes of incest, murder, and rebellion unfolded in his family life.

David's sin of adultery and murder constituted a perfect crime from the human perspective. It was a time of military success and empire expansion. The Philistines were subservient and the Aramean-Ammonite coalition had been broken the previous year. While David remained in Jerusalem, the Israelite armies under the command of Joab were sent to conquer the Ammonite city of Rabbah. Being enticed by Bathsheba, David committed adultery. He knew that she was the wife of Uriah, the Hittite, a loyal mercenary in the army of Israel. The king recalled Uriah from the front line but then sent him back to Job with a letter arranging for him to be killed in battle by the enemy. When reports came to Jerusalem that Uriah had fallen in an Ammonite battle, David married Bathsheba. Perhaps the facts of David's heinous crime were concealed, since a frontline casualty was a common occurrence. Even if this was known to Joab, who was he to challenge or reprove the king?

Although David was responsible to no one in the kingdom, he failed to realize that this "perfect crime" was known to God. For a despot in a heathen nation adultery and murder might have passed unchallenged, but this could not be so in Israel, where a king held his position as a sacred trust. When Nathan depicted David's crime in the dramatic story of the rich man who took advantage of his poor servant, David became enraged that such injustice might prevail under his jurisdiction. Nathan boldly declared that David was the man guilty of murder and adultery. Fortunately for Nathan, the king repented. David's spiritual crisis found lofty expression in poetry (Pss. 32 and 51). He was granted forgiveness, but grave, indeed, were the domestic consequences (2 Sam. 12:11).

Immorality and murder within the famimly soon involved David in civil strife and rebellion. David's lack of discipline and restraint set a poor example for his sons. Amnon's immoral behavior with his half-sister resulted in his assassination by Absalom, another son of David. Naturally Absalom incurred the disfavor of his father. As a result he found it expedient to leave Jerusalem, taking refuge with Talmai, his grandfather, in Geshur. Here he remained for three years.

Joab, commander of David's army, was able to effect reconciliation between father and son. Soon after this, however, Absalom staged a rebellion at Hebron, taking David by surprise. Being a brilliant militarist David fled Jerusalem but ultimately put Absalom's armies to flight. Another rebellion led by Sheba was likewise suppressed, and David was restored to Jerusalem as king.

For nearly a decade of David's reign the solemn words spoken by Nathan were realistically fulfilled. Beginning with Amnon's immorality and continuing to the suppression of Sheba's rebellion, evil had fermented in David's own house (2 Sam. 11:1–20:26).

David's military and civil organization of the kingdom developed gradually throughout his reign as the empire expanded. The basic pattern of organization may have been similar to Egyptian practice. Among high officials were the chronicler, who was in charge of public relations, and the scribe, or secretary, who was in charge of domestic and foreign correspondence and accordingly had a hand in matters of diplomacy. Matters of judgment were handled by the king himself (2 Sam. 14:4–17; cf. 1 Chron 26:29–27:34).

David chose Mount Moriah as the site for the building of the Temple under his son Solomon and made elaborate plans and detailed arrangements. Publicly he charged Solomon with the responsibility of obeying the law as it had been given through Moses.

The last words of David (2 Sam. 23:1–7) reveal the greatness of Israel's most honored hero. Another song (2 Sam. 22), expressing his thanksgiving and praise for a life replete with great victories and deliverances, may have been composed in the closing years of his life and closely associated with this poem. Here he speaks prophetically about the eternal endurance of his kingdom. God had spoken to him, affirming an everlasting covenant. This testimony by David would have made a fitting epitaph for his tomb.

The Golden Era of Solomon

Peace and prosperity characterize the reign of Solomon. David had established the kingdom; Solomon reaped the benefits of his father's labors. Brief is the account of his reign as given in 1 Kings 1:1–11:43 and 2 Chronicles 1:1–9:31.

In spite of opposition by other contenders for the throne, Solomon was acclaimed as king of Israel at an early age, possibly in his early twenties. At Gibeon, where the tabernacle was located, he offered sacrifice and made his request for divine wisdom.

Although little information is given about the organization of his vast empire, it is known that Solomon divided his kingdom into twelve districts for purposes of taxation. He maintained a large army, including a fighting force of fourteen hundred chariots and twelve thousand horsemen, which he stationed in Jerusalem and the chariot cities throughout the nation.

Most important in the vast and extensive building program of Solomon was the Temple. Treaty arrangements made by David with Hiram, king of Tyre, were continued by Solomon so that the Phoenicians supplied architects and technicians, as well as workmen, for building the Temple in Jerusalem. This Temple in all its beauty and splendor was completed in about seven years.

For the dedication of the Temple the Israelites assembled to observe the Feast of Tabernacles, vividly reminding them of their wilderness pilgrimage. Solomon was the key person in the dedication ceremonies. With all Israelites as servants and priests of God (Lev. 25:42, 55; Jer. 30:10; Exod. 19:6), Solomon took the position of a servant of God, representing the nation chosen by God to be his people. This servant relationship was common to prophet, priest, and layman, as well as the king, in true recognition of human dignity. In this capacity Solomon offered prayer, delivered the dedicatory address, and officiated at the offering of sacrifices.

In the religious history of Israel the dedication of the Temple was the most significant event since the people had left Sinai. The sudden transformation from slavery in Egypt to an independent nation in the wilderness was a momentous demonstration of God's power in behalf of his nation. At that time the tabernacle was erected to aid them in their recognition and service of God. Now the Temple had been erected under Solomon. As the presence of God was visibly manifested in the pillar of cloud over the tabernacle (Exod. 40:34; Lev. 9:23-24), so the glory of God hovered over the Temple and signified God's blessing and benediction. This divinely confirmed the establishment of the kingdom as anticipated by Moses (Deut. 17:14-20).

Solomon also built a palace for himself, which was thirteen years in building but only briefly noted in the biblical record. His powerful standing army also required much building throughout the kingdom. Mining operations in the Wadi Arabah, his seaport at Elath on the Gulf of Aqaba, and his favorable relations with the Phoenicians opened opportunities for trade with distant points in the Mediterranean such as Spain and the African coast of Ethiopia.

King Solomon gained such international respect and recognition that his wealth was greatly increased by gifts from far and near. In answer to his initial request he had been divinely endowed with wisdom, so that people from other lands came to hear his proverbs, his songs, and his speeches on various subjects (1 Kings 4:29-34). If the account of the visit by the queen of Sheba is but a sample of what happened frequently during Solomon's reign, then one can see that gold became plentiful in Israel's capital. The fact that the queen traveled over twelve hundred miles by camel may also have been motivated by commercial interests. The naval expeditions from Ezion-geber may have stimulated negotiations for favorable trade agreements. Her mission was quite successful (1 Kings 10:13). Although Solomon, in addition to granting her requests, returned to her all that she had brought, it is doubtful that he did the same for all the kings and governors of Arabia who brought gifts to him (2 Chron. 9:12-14). While it is difficult to ascertain the value of the wealth described here, there is no doubt that Solomon represented the epitome in wealth and wisdom of all the kings who ruled in Jerusalem.

The final chapter of Solomon's reign is tragic (1 Kings 11). Why the king of Israel, who reached the zenith of success in wisdom, wealth, fame, and international acclaim under divine blessing, should terminate his forty-year reign under omens of failure is most perplexing! Consequently some have regarded the record as unreliable and contradictory and have sought other explanations. The truth of the matter is that Solomon, who played the leading role at the dedication of the Temple, departed from wholehearted devotion to God—an experience parallel to that of Israel in the wilderness after building the tabernacle. Solomon broke the very first commandment by his policy of allowing idol worship in Jerusalem.

Intermarriage between royal families was a common practice in the Near East when alliances were made between nations. Whether Solomon's marriages were motivated by diplomatic and political expediency to ensure peace and safety or by an attempt to surpass sovereigns of other nations, whose luxury was expressed in a large harem, is not indicated. Nevertheless it was contrary to the expressed commands of God (Deut. 17:17). Solomon permitted the multiplicity of wives to be his ruination by allowing his heart to be turned away from God.

Solomon not only tolerated idolatry, but he himself gave recognition to Ashtoreth, the fertility goddess of the Phoenicians, who was known as Astarte among the Greeks and Ishtar among the Babylonians. For the worship of Milcom, or Molech, Solomon erected a high place on a mountain east of Jerusalem. These were not removed for three and a half centuries, but remained as an abomination in the proximity of the Temple until the days of Josiah (2 Kings 23:13).

Idolatry, a violation of the opening words of the Decalogue (Exod. 20), could not be tolerated. God's rebuff was probably delivered through the prophet Ahijah, who appears later in this chapter. Because of his disobedience the kingdom of Israel was to be divided. The dynasty of David would continue to rule over part of the kingdom for the sake of David, with whom God had made a covenant, and because of Jerusalem, which God had chosen. God would not break his covenantal promise, even though Solomon had forfeited his blessings and favor, so temporary judgment was in the offing. Also, for David's sake, the kingdom would not be disrupted during Solomon's lifetime, but adversaries would arise to threaten peace and safety before the termination of his reign.

In Edom Hadad rose to power before Solomon's death and threatened Israel's resources and lucrative Arabian trade and commerce on the Red Sea. Rezon of Damascus posed a greater threat when he formed an independent Aramaean kingdom with commercial and political consequences for Israel. As matters turned out, one of Solomon's own men—Jeroboam, son of Nebat—proved to be the real disruptive factor in Israel. Through a symbolic act Ahijah, the prophet, conveyed to Jeroboam, who had gained a following in Israel, that he would be entrusted with rule over ten tribes of Israel. With his life endangered, Jeroboam fled to Egypt for safety until after Solomon's death.

Solomon was subjected to the anguish of rebellion at home and secession in various parts of his realm before he died. As a result of his personal failure to obey and serve God wholeheartedly, the general welfare and peaceful prosperity of the kingdom were endangered.

For additional study help see *Figures* 5 and 6 in the Appendix.

Chapter 7

THE KINGDOM DIVIDED

The two kingdoms arising after Solomon's death are commonly differentiated by the appellations "Northern" and "Southern." The latter designates the smaller state, ruled by the Davidic dynasty from its capital at Jerusalem until 586 B.C. It consisted of the tribes of Judah and Benjamin, who supported Rehoboam with an army when the rest of the tribes seceded in rebellion against the oppressive measures of Solomon and his son (1 Kings 12:21). The "Northern Kingdom" designates the seceding tribes, who made Jeroboam their king. This kingdom endured until 722 B.C. with its capital successively at Shechem, Tirzah, and Samaria.

The common biblical designations for these two kingdoms are "Israel" and "Judah." The former usually is restricted in its use to the Northern Kingdom, while the latter refers to the Southern Kingdom. Originally the name "Israel" was given to Jacob (Gen. 32:-22–32). During his lifetime it was already applied to his sons (Gen. 44:7), and ever since then any descendant of Jacob has been properly referred to as an "Israelite." From patriarchal times to the occupation of Canaan, "Israel" specified the whole Hebrew nation. This designation prevailed throughout the monarchy of David and Solomon, even though there was a divided rule in the early part of David's reign.

The tribe of Judah, which was strategically located and exceptionally strong, came into prominence during the time of Saul (see 1 Sam. 11:8, etc.). After the division in 931 B.C. the name "Judah" identified the Southern Kingdom, which continued its allegiance to the Davidic dynasty. Unless otherwise indicated, the names "Israel" and "Judah" in this volume represent the Northern and Southern Kingdoms, respectively.

Another appellation for the Northern Kingdom is "Ephraim." Although this name originally was given to one of the sons of Joseph (Gen. 41:52), it specifically designated the leading tribe of secession. Being located to the north of Benjamin and Judah, "Ephraim" represented the opposition to Judah and often included the whole Northern Kingdom (see Isaiah and Hosea).

Chronology

The most thorough study of chronology for this period of the divided kingdom is published in a book by E. R. Thiele, *The Mysterious Numbers of the Hebrew Kings*. Basic to his study were the eponym list that accounts for every year in Assyrian history from 891 to 648 B.C. and Ptolemy's canon listing the Babylonian and Persian rulers from the time of Nabonassar, 747 B.C., to Darius III, 332 B.C. Two significant facts furnish the link between Assyrian history and the biblical account. Assyrian inscriptions indicate that Ahab, king of Israel, participated in the battle of Karkar (853 B.C.) against Shalmaneser III, and that Jehu, another king of Israel, paid tribute to the same Assyrian king in 841 B.C. By equating the biblical data concerning the Hebrew kings Ahaziah and Joram to this twelve-year period of Assyrian history, Thiele has suggested a clue to the proper chronology. With these two dates definitely established in the synchronism between Assyrian and Hebrew history, he proposes a scheme of absolute chronology for the period from the disruption of the kingdom to the fall of Jerusalem. This serves as a practical key to the interpretation of the numerous chronological references in the accounts of Kings and Chronicles. Based on this study, Thiele dates the Northern Kingdom from 931 to 722 B.C. and the Southern Kingdom from 931 to 586 B.C. A suggested working chronology for this period in simplified form is as follows:

931—Dynasty of Jeroboam I   Rehoboam
909—Dynasty of Baasha
885—Dynasty of Omri   Jehoshaphat
841—Dynasty of Jehu
752—Last Kings   Uzziah
722—Fall of Samaria
                             Hezekiah
640—   Josiah
586—   Fall of Jerusalem

By using these suggested dates as a working scheme, the problem of chronological data in the biblical account can be reduced to a minimum. While dates for each king become significant in a detailed study, the dates in this scheme are sufficient for an understanding of the general developments.

Biblical Account

The primary literary source for the divided kingdom era is 1 Kings 11:1 to 2 Kings 25:30 and 2 Chronicles 10:1–36:23. The latter continues the account of David's dynasty, whose genealogy is traced back to Adam (1 Chron. 1:1). Supplementary material may be found in Isaiah, Jeremiah, and other prophets reflecting contemporary culture.

The only source presenting a continuous historical account of the Northern Kingdom is 1 Kings 12:1 through 2 Kings 17:41. Integrated in this record are contemporaneous events in the Southern Kingdom. With the Northern Kingdom terminating in 722 B.C., the author of Kings continues the running account of the Southern Kingdom in 2 Kings 18:1–25:30 to the fall of Jerusalem in 586 B.C. A parallel record for the Southern Kingdom from 931 to 586 B.C. is given in 2 Chronicles 10:1–36:23, where the author concludes with a closing reference to the release from captivity under Cyrus (ca. 538 B.C.). The account in Chronicles supplements the Northern Kingdom history recorded in the Books of Kings only where it has a direct bearing on developments in the Southern Kingdom.

Concurrent Events

International relations are vitally significant during these centuries when the Solomonic empire divided into two kingdoms—which finally succumbed to foreign powers. Being strategically located in the Fertile Crescent between Egypt and Mesopotamia, they could not escape the pressure of various nations that rose to great power during this period. Consequently, for a proper understanding of the biblical history, these nations warrant consideration.

The Kingdom of Aram (Syria)

The kingdom of Aram, with Damascus as its capital, is better known as Syria. For about two centuries it enjoyed power and prosperity at the expense of Israel. When David expanded his kingdom he defeated Hadadezer, ruler of Zobah, and established amity with Toi, king of Hamath. Solomon extended the frontier of his kingdom over a hundred miles beyond Damascus and Zobah, conquering Hamath on the Orontes and establishing store cities in that area. During the latter part of his reign, Rezon, who had been a young military officer under Hadadezer at Zobah prior to his defeat by David, seized Damascus and laid the foundation for the rise of the Aramaean, or Syrian, kingdom. Rebellion under Rehoboam provided this opportunity. For the next two centuries Aram became a contender for power in the Syro-Palestinian area.

War between Judah and the Northern Kingdom, with Asa and Baasha as respective rulers, afforded Syria, under Benhadad, the opportunity to emerge as the strongest nation in Canaan near the end of the ninth century B.C. When Baasha began to fortify the border city of Ramah, only five miles north of Jerusalem, Asa sent temple treasures up to Benhadad as a bribe, making an alliance with him against Israel. Although this accomplished Asa's immediate purpose and relieved him of the military pressure from Baasha, it in reality gave Syria the upper hand, so that both Hebrew kingdoms were in time threatened by invasion from the north. By taking possession of some of the northern territory in Israel, Benhadad was able to control the caravan routes to Phoenicia, which brought immense wealth to Damascus—strengthening the kingdom of Syria.

The supremacy of Syria as a military and commercial power was tempered by the Northern Kingdom when the dynasty of Omri began to rule in 885 B.C. Omri broke Syria's commercial monopoly with Phoenicia by establishing friendly relations with Ethbaal, king of Sidon. This resulted in the marriage of Jezebel and Ahab. The rising power of Assyria on the east served as another check on Syria in the days of Ahab. During the years that Ashurnasirpal, king of Assyria, was content to bypass Syria to the north in extending his contact to the Mediterranean, Ahab and Benhadad frequently opposed each other. In the course of time Ahab gained the balance of power. In 853 B.C., however, Ahab and Benhadad united their forces in the famous battle of Karkar in the Orontes valley, north of Hamath. Although Shalmaneser III claimed a great victory, it is doubtful whether it was decisive, since he did not advance to Hamath or Damascus until several years later. Immediately after this battle, Syro-Ephraimitic hostility continued, Ahab being killed in battle (1 Kings 22). As Assyria renewed attacks on Syria, Benhadad may not have had the support of Joram of the Northern Kingdom. When Benhadad died, about 843 B.C., Syria was hard pressed by the Assyrian invaders as well as the lack of support from the Northern Kingdom.

Hazael, the next ruler, usurped the throne and became one of the most powerful kings—extending Syria's domain into Palestine. Although Jehu, the new king in Israel, submitted to Shalmaneser III by paying him taxes (841 B.C.), Hazael withstood the invasion of the Assyrian king single-handed. In a few years Hazael was able to enlarge his kingdom when the Assyrians withdrew. Extensive territory was annexed from the Northern Kingdom at Jehu's expense. After 814 B.C. Jehoahaz, king of Israel, was so weak that Hazael's armies passed through his territory and took possession of the Philistine plain, destroying Gath and exacting tribute from the king of Judah in Jerusalem.

Benhadad (ca. 801 B.C.) failed to maintain the kingdom established by his father Hazael. During the last few years of his reign, Adadnirari III of Assyria subdued Damascus sufficiently to exact a heavy tribute. Besides this, Benhadad faced hostile opposition from Syrian states to the north. This left Damascus in such a weakened position that when the Assyrian pressure continued Jehoash reclaimed for Israel much of the territory taken by Hazael. In the days of Jeroboam II (793–753 B.C.) Syria even lost Damascus and the "approaches to Hamath," restoring the northern boundary held by David and Solomon (2 Sam. 8:5–11).

Damascus once more had an opportunity to assert itself when the powerful Jeroboam II died in 753 B.C. Rezin (ca. 750–732 B.C.), the last of the Aramaean kings at Damascus, regained Syrian independence. With the accession of Tiglath-pileser III to the Assyrian throne (745 B.C.) both Syria and Israel were subject to invasion and heavy tribute. While Tiglath-pileser III (Pul) was fighting in Armenia (737–735 B.C.), Rezin and Pekah organized an alliance to avoid payment of tribute. Although Edom and Philistia joined Syria and Israel in this anti-Assyrian alliance, Ahaz, king of Judah, sent tribute to Pul, pledging his allegiance. In response to this invitation Pul made a campaign against Philistia, establishing contact with Ahaz, and by 732 had conquered Damascus. Samaria was saved at this time when Pekah was replaced by Hoshea, who willingly paid tribute as a puppet king. With the death of Rezin and the fall of Damascus, the kingdom of Syria came to its end, never to rise again.

The Great Assyrian Empire

In the northeast corner of the Fertile Crescent, stretching some 350 miles along the Tigris River at an approximate width of 200 miles, is the land known as Assyria. The name probably comes from the national god, Ashur, after whom one of its leading cities was named. The importance of Assyria during the divided kingdom period is immediately apparent in the fact that at the height of its power it absorbed the kingdoms of Syria, Israel, Judah, and even Egypt as far as Thebes. For approximately two and a half centuries it exerted a tremendous influence upon developments in the land of Canaan and therefore frequently appears in the biblical record.

Assyrian history proper had its beginnings about 1100 B.C. with the reign of Tiglath-pileser I (1114–1076 B.C.). According to his annals, he extended the power of his nation westward to the Mediterranean Sea, overpowering the small and weaker nations in that area. However, during the next two centuries Assyrian power recedes into the background while Israel, under David and Solomon, rises to a dominant power in the Fertile Crescent.

Beginning with the ninth century Assyria emerges as a rising power. Assyrian eponym lists from about 892 to 648 B.C. make it possible to correlate and integrate the history of Assyria with the developments in Israel as recorded in the biblical account. Ashurnasirpal II (883–859 B.C.) established Calah as his capital. After developing strong military power he began pushing westward, terrorizing the opposing nations with his ruthlessness and cruelty, crossing the Euphrates, and establishing commercial contacts on the Mediterranean. Frequent contacts with the Syrians to the south brought on an important battle at Karkar on the Orontes River in 853 B.C. in the days of his son Shalmaneser III (858–824 B.C.). In the coalition headed by Benhadad of Damascus, Ahab, king of Israel, furnished two thousand chariots and ten thousand soldiers, constituting the largest unit in this group. Although the Assyrian king claimed the victory, it is doubtful whether it was decisive, since Shalmaneser III avoided contact with the Syrians for several years after this. In 848 B.C., and again in 845, Benhadad resisted two more Assyrian invasions, but no mention is made of any Israelite forces aiding the Syrians at this time. Jehu, who usurped the throne in Samaria at this time (841 B.C.), made subservient overtures to Shalmaneser III by sending him tribute. This left Hazael, the new king in Damascus, with the problem of resisting Assyrian aggression. Although Shalmaneser harassed Syria for a few years in the days of Hazael, he found it expedient to turn his attention to the conquest of areas in the north after 837 B.C., giving Canaan relief from Assyrian pressure for several decades.

For nearly a century Assyrian power fades into the background. Shamshi-Adad V (823–811 B.C.) was kept busy suppressing revolts in various parts of the kingdom. Adadnirari III (810–783) attacked Damascus before the turn of the century, relieving the Israelites from oppression by Syria. Shalmaneser IV (782–773), Ashurdan III (772–755), and Ashurnirari (754–745) successfully maintained Assyria as a powerful nation but were not strong enough to enlarge it, as did the following ruler.

Tiglath-pileser III (745–727 B.C.) was an outstanding warrior who led his nation in further conquests. In Babylon, where he was recognized as king, he was known as Pul (cf. 2 Kings 15:19). He divided conquered areas into subject provinces for more control and became notoriously effective in terrorizing the nations by exchanging large groups of people in a conquered city with captives from a distant area. This checked the possibility of rebellion and served as a leveling process linguistically, so that the Aramaic language displaced others in the large kingdom area. At the beginning of his reign Pul exacted tribute from Menahem, king of Israel, and Rezin, king of Damascus. Since Judah was the strongest nation in Canaan at this time, it is possible that Azariah may have organized a coalition of forces to oppose the Assyrians. It seems that his successors, Jotham and Ahaz, resisted pressure from Israel and Syria to join them, as well as Philistia and Edom, in opposing Pul. Instead Ahaz issued friendly overtures to Pul, in response to which the Assyrian forces advanced as far as Philistia in 733 B.C., possessing territory at the expense of these opposing nations. After a terrible siege, the great city of Damascus fell, Rezin was killed, and the Syrian kingdom capitulated. Samaria averted conquest by replacing Pekah with Hoshea.

Shalmaneser V (727–722 B.C.) carried on his father's policies. In the days of Hoshea the Israelites were anxious to terminate their subservience to Assyria. Shalmaneser responded with an invasion of

Israel, and for three years besieged Samaria. In 722 B.C. Sargon II, who served as a general in the army, usurped the throne and founded a new dynasty in Assyria. In the records he claims that he captured Samaria, although some believe that Shalmaneser really took the city and Sargon claimed the credit. Ruling from 721 to 705 B.C., he used Ashur, Calah, and Nineveh as capitals, but finally built the great city of Khorsabad for which he is best remembered. His campaign against Ashdod in 711 may be the one mentioned in Isaiah 20:1. Sargon's reign was abruptly terminated by his death in battle.

Sennacherib (704–681 B.C.) made the city of Nineveh famous as his great capital by building a wall some forty to fifty feet high around a 2.5-mile length along the Tigris River. In his annals he lists the conquest of Sidon, Joppa, and forty-six walled cities in Judah, and his assault on Jerusalem in the days of Hezekiah. In 681 he was killed by two of his sons.

Although Sennacherib had been stopped at the borders of Egypt, his son Esarhaddon (681–668 B.C.) advanced into Egypt and defeated Taharka. His interest in Babylonia is evidenced by his rebuilding of the city of Babylon, possibly because his wife was of the Babylonian nobility. Sennacherib appointed Shamash-shum-ukin as ruler of Babylon, but the latter rebelled, after a sixteen-year rule, against his brother Ashurbanipal and perished in the burning of Babylon (648 B.C.). During Esarhaddon's reign, Manasseh, king of Judah, was taken captive to Babylon (2 Chron. 33:10–13). Death came to Esarhaddon as he was marching his armies to Egypt.

During the reign of Ashurbanipal (668–ca. 630 B.C.), the Assyrian empire reached its zenith in wealth and prestige. In Egypt he marched his armies some five hundred miles up the Nile to capture Thebes in 663 B.C. Civil War (652 B.C.) with his brother, who was in charge of Babylon, resulted in the capture of that city in 648. Although he was cruel and ruthless as a military general, Ashurbanipal is best remembered for his keen interest in religious, scientific, and literary works. Sending scribes all over Assyria and Babylonia to copy records of creation, floods, ancient history, and the like, he amassed much material in the great royal library of Nineveh.

In less than three three decades after Ashurbanipal's death the Assyrian kingdom, which had exerted such tremendous influence throughout the Fertile Crescent, faded away—never to rise again. The three succeeding rulers were unable to cope with the rising kingdoms in Media and Babylonia. Nineveh fell in 612 B.C. With the battles of Haran (609) and Carchemish (605 B.C.) the last vestige of Assyrian opposition disappeared. Expanding westward, the Babylonian kingdom absorbed the Southern Kingdom and destroyed Jerusalem in 586 B.C.

For additional study help see *Figures 7* and *8* in the Appendix.

Chapter 8

THE NORTHERN KINGDOM

The union of Israel established by David terminated with Solomon's death. Foremost in the resultant division was the Northern Kingdom—located between Judah and Syria. Three dynasties ruled during the first ninety years (931–841 B.C.) Under the dynasty of Jehu, for the next almost ninety years (841–753 B.C.), the Northern Kingdom reached its zenith in territorial and economic expansion and political power. During the next three decades Israel disintegrated under a number of weaker kings and capitulated to Assyrian conquest in 722 B.C.

The Royal Family of Jeroboam—1 Kings 12:25–14:20; 15:25–31

Jeroboam, a distinguished administrator who fell into disfavor with Solomon and fled to Egypt for safety, was welcomed back to champion the cause of the tribes who rebelled against Rehoboam when he acceded to his father's throne in Jerusalem. Assembled at Shechem, the elders of the seceding tribes made Jeroboam their king.

As king of Israel Jeroboam took the initiative in religious matters. Naturally he did not want his people to attend the sacred festivities at Jerusalem, lest they turn their allegiance to Rehoboam. By erecting golden calves at Dan and Bethel, he instituted idolatry in Israel (2 Chron. 11:13–15). He appointed priests freely, ignoring Mosaic restrictions and allowing Israelites to offer sacrifices at various high places throughout the land. As chief priest he not only officiated at the altar but also changed one of the feast days from the seventh to the eighth month (1 Kings 12:25–13:34).

His aggressiveness in religious matters was tempered when he was warned by a prophet from Judah. Ahijah, the prophet who had informed him that he would be king, also continued to make Jeroboam conscious of his accountability to God. In spite of all these prophetic warnings Jeroboam continued in idolatry. Civil strife undoubtedly so weakened Israel that Jeroboam even lost the city of Bethel to Judah in the days of Abijah, the son of Rehoboam. After his 22-year reign he was succeeded by his son Nadab, who ruled less than two years before he was assassinated by Baasha.

Baasha's Dynasty—1 Kings 15:32–16:20

Baasha established himself as king over Israel at Tirzah. Chronic war with Judah prevailed throughout his 22-year reign over Israel. When he attempted to fortify Ramah, located only five miles north of Jerusalem, Asa, king of Judah, scored a diplomatic victory by renewing his alliance with Benhadad I of Damascus, who took possession of cities in northern Israel. Baasha abandoned the fortification of Ramah, thus alleviating the threat to Jerusalem.

The prophet Jehu, son of Hanani, admonished Baasha to serve God. Unfortunately he ignored the prophet's advice and continued in the sinful ways of Jeroboam. His son Elah succeeded him but was killed by Zimri, who was in charge of half the royal chariots. After he killed all the relatives of this royal family, Zimri, fearing lack of support by Omri, who was in charge of Israelite troops, in desperation secluded himself in the royal palace, which he then reduced to ashes. Thus ended his seven-day reign.

The Omride Rulers—1 Kings 16:21–2 Kings 9:37

Omri, founder of the most notorious dynasty in Israel, has only eight verses allotted to him for his twelve-year reign. He built the city of Samaria and established the international prestige of the Northern

Kingdom by promoting friendly alliances with surrounding nations. Samaria was the new site for his capital and became a lasting monument to his rule. Strategically located seven miles northwest of Shechem on the road leading to Phoenicia, Galilee, and Esdraelon, Samaria was secured as the impregnable capital of Israel for over a century and a half, until it was conquered by the Assyrians in 722 B.C.

Omri's policy of friendship with Phoenicia—a policy previously promoted by David and Solomon—was fundamentally significant for Israel's commercial expansion. This alliance was sealed in the marriage of his son Ahab and Jezebel, the daughter of Ethbaal, king of the Sidonians, which undoubtedly initiated a policy of religious syncretism.

Moab, according to the Moabite stone discovered in 1868 and now located in the Louvre Museum in Paris, was made subject to Omri. By collecting tribute and controlling trade, Israel gained great wealth.

The warfare that had prevailed between Israel and Judah during the two preceding dynasties very likely was replaced by friendly overtures. This culminated in intermarriage between the royal families in the next generation.

Relations with Syria in the days of Omri very likely were in tension as he gained control of the wealthy caravan routes westward to Accho on the Mediterranean coast through his treaty with Phoenicia. Being a shrewd militarist and diplomat, he may have had some contact with Assyria, which certainly would have tempered the Syrian attitude toward Israel.

Ahab successfully expanded the political and commercial interest of Israel during his 22-year reign (874–853 B.C.). Although increasing commerce with Phoenicia represented a serious threat to the lucrative trading interest of Syria, Ahab avoided open warfare while he secured the welfare of Israel.

Throughout his kingdom Ahab built and fortified many cities, including Jericho. Exacting heavy tribute in livestock from Moab, he gained a favorable balance of trade with Phoenicia and Syria. With Judah he ensured friendship with the marriage of his daughter, Athaliah, to Jehoram, son of Jehoshaphat (ca. 865 B.C.). The support of Judah strengthened Israel against Syria. By maintaining peace and developing a lucrative trade, Ahab was able to continue the building program in Samaria. The wealth he lavished on himself is indicated in 1 Kings 22:39, where reference is made to his palace "inlaid with ivory." The ivory discovered by archaeologists in the ruins of Samaria may well be from Ahab's time.

Promoting idol worship, Ahab built a temple to Baal in this great capital city of Samaria. Hundreds of prophets were brought into Israel to make Baalism the religion of Ahab's people. In view of this, Ahab earned the reputation of being the most sinful of all kings who had ruled Israel.

Elijah was God's messenger in this era of rank apostasy. Emerging suddenly from Gilead to challenge this king of Israel, Elijah announced a drought and then secluded himself under divine instructions. Returning to meet Ahab after the drought had lasted a three and a half years, Elijah was charged with being a "troubler of Israel." With Ahab and 950 of his prophets of Baal and Asherah present at Mount Carmel, Elijah confronted the Israelites with the fact that they could not serve God and Baal at the same time. In a dramatic demonstration Elijah's prayer was answered as "the fire of the Lord burned up the sacrifice" and the people acknowledged that "the LORD, he is God!"

Threatened by Jezebel, Elijah fled to Mount Horeb in the Sinai desert. There God commissioned him to anoint Hazael as king of Syria and Jehu as king over Israel, and to call Elisha as his successor. On his return to Israel Elisha became his co-worker.

By effective diplomacy and favorable treaties Ahab was able to maintain peaceful relations with surrounding countries until the latter part of his reign. By his brilliant strategy, Ahab in time defeated and captured Benhadad, the Syrian king. Ahab released him and even allowed him to state his own peace terms; some cities were restored to Israel, and trading rights were granted to the victors in Damascus. This gracious and generous treatment of Israel's worst enemy was part of Ahab's foreign policy of establishing friendly alliances with surrounding nations. Ahab may have anticipated Assyrian aggression, so that the treaty of Aphek represented his plan to retain Syria as a friendly buffer state.

Ahab failed to acknowledge God in this significant victory. En route to Samaria, a prophet dramatically reminded him that an ordinary soldier forfeits his life for disobedience. How much more so the king of Israel who had not fulfilled his commission when God granted him victory. The prophet's ominous warning spoiled Ahab's victory celebration.

The final encounter between Elijah and Ahab took place in the vineyard the ruthless Jezebel had acquired by having Naboth publicly condemned and stoned. Boldly Elijah indicted Ahab for shedding innocent blood. For this gross injustice the Omride dynasty was doomed to destruction. Even though Ahab repented, this judgment was tempered only by postponement until after his death.

Although not mentioned in Scripture, the battle of Karkar (853 B.C.), occurring during the three-year, truce between Syria and Israel (1 Kings 22:1), was significant enough to warrant detailed consideration in Assyrian annals. After taking numerous cities north of Karkar in their advance toward the Mediterranean, the Assyrians were halted by a strong coalition at Karkar. Although Shalmaneser claimed victory, the Assyrians did not resume their advance to Hamath during the next five or six years.

Later that year Ahab, joined by King Jehoshaphat from Judah, was engaged in battle with Syria trying to recover Aphek and oust the Syrians from Gilead. In this battle Ahab was killed, as predicted by the prophets Elijah and Micaiah (1 Kings 21–22). He was succeeded by his son Ahaziah, who reigned approximately one year.

Joram, another son of Ahab and Jezebel, began his twelve-year reign in 852 B.C. as the last king in the Omride dynasty. One of his first problems was the Moabite rebellion. Although the kings of Judah and Edom marched with him against Moab, they returned to Israel without resubjugating Moab.

Warfare between Israel and Syria was carried on intermittently during the reign of Joram. Benhadad even encamped his army around the city of Samaria, subjecting the city to famine. Elisha had an interesting ministry throughout this period, in which Joram and his people were miraculously delivered from these invading Syrians.

Elisha's ministry was known not only throughout Israel but in Syria as well as in Judah and Edom. Through the healing of Naaman and the peculiar encounter of the Syrian armies with this prophet, Elisha was recognized as the "man of God" even in Damascus, the Syrian capital. Toward the end of Joram's reign Elisha made a visit to Damascus (2 Kings 8:7–15), where he informed Hazael, a servant of King Benhadad, that he would succeed his master as king of Syria. Shortly after this Hazael smothered the ailing king and seized the Syrian throne.

With the change of kings on the Syrian throne, Joram made an attempt to recover Ramoth Gilead. Although Joram captured this strategic fortress, he was wounded in the battle. While he was recuperating at Jezreel, his nephew Ahaziah, king of Judah, went to visit him. At this time Jehu was in charge of the Israelite army stationed in Ramoth Gilead.

Elisha once more comes into focus on the national scene as he performs the other unfulfilled mission given to Elijah at Mount Horeb. This time Elijah did not go himself but sent one of his followers to Ramoth Gilead to anoint Jehu as king of Israel. Jehu was charged with the responsibility of avenging the blood of the prophets and servants of the Lord. The family of Ahab and Jezebel was to be exterminated as the dynasties of Jeroboam and Baasha had been before Omri.

With the blowing of the trumpet Jehu was proclaimed king. In a quick assault on Jezreel, Joram was fatally wounded and thrown on the plot of ground Ahab had taken at the expense of Naboth's blood, fulfilling Elijah's prediction. Ahaziah attempted to flee but was also mortally wounded. He died at Megiddo and was taken to Jerusalem for burial. Although Jezebel made an appeal to Jehu, she was ruthlessly thrown out of a window to her death. Her body was eaten by dogs. Judgment thus came upon the dynasty of Omri, literally fulfilling the words of the prophet Elijah.

The Jehu Dynasty—2 Kings 10:1–15:12

Jehu, an army captain, came to the throne in Israel through a bloody revolution in 841 B.C. Marching to Samaria he slew seventy sons of Ahab's family and directed the execution of all the Baal zealots who had been inveigled into mass celebrations in the temple erected by Ahab. Since religion and politics had been so intimately fused in the Omride dynasty, the ruthless destruction of Baalism was a matter of expediency for Jehu.

Jehu was troubled on every hand. By exterminating the Omride dynasty he forfeited the favor of Judah and Phoenicia, whose royal families were closely allied with Jezebel. Nor did he join the new Syrian king, Hazael, in opposing the Assyrian westward advance.

On the famous Black Obelisk discovered by Layard in 1846, Shalmaneser III reports that he received tribute from Jehu. After five unsuccessful attacks on Damascus, the Assyrian king marched his armies to the Mediterranean coast and collected tribute from Tyre and Sidon as well as from the king of Israel. By this conciliatory move, Jehu warded off an Assyrian invasion of Israel, but he incurred the antagonism of Hazael by placating Shalmaneser III. During the early years of this period (841–837 B.C.) Hazael resisted Assyrian aggression single-handedly. The Assyrians did not renew their attacks for almost two decades. This allowed Hazael to direct his well-seasoned military might southward in a renewal of the war with Israel. At Jehu's expense the Syrians occupied the land of Gilead and Bashan, east of Jordan. Having come to the throne by means of a bloody insurrection, Jehu apparently never unified his nation sufficiently to withstand Hazael's might. It is doubtful whether Hazael reduced Jehu to Syrian vassalage, but for the rest of Jehu's days Israel was harassed and troubled by this aggressive Syrian king.

Although Jehu did away with Baalism he did not conform to the law of God. Idolatry still prevailed from Dan to Bethel—therefore the divine warning that his sons would reign after him only to the fourth generation.

Jehoahaz, son of Jehu, had the same Syrian king to reckon with throughout his reign (814–798 B.C.). Hazael took advantage of the new ruler in Israel by extending the Syrian domain into the hill country of Ephraim. He even advanced beyond Israel to capture Gath and threatened to conquer Jerusalem (2 Kings 12:17). Israel was so weakened that such nations as the Edomites, Ammonites, Philistines, and Tyrians took advantage of Israel's plight (cf. Amos 1:6–15; Isa. 9:12). Under the pressure of foreign oppression Jehoahaz turned to God—and Israel was not completely overrun by the Syrians. In spite of this relief he did not depart from Jeroboam's idolatry; nor did he destroy the asherim in Samaria (2 Kings 13:1–9).

Jehoash, the third king in the Jehu dynasty, ruled Israel for sixteen years (798–782 B.C.). With the death of Hazael, shortly before the turn of the century, he found it possible to begin the restoration of Israel's fortunes. The prophet Elisha, who had performed so many miracles, especially during reign of Joram, was still living when Jehoash ascended the throne. The silence of the Scriptures warrants the conclusion that neither Jehu nor Jehoahaz had much to do with Elisha. On his deathbed Elisha dramatically assured Jehoash that he would defeat the Syrians. The final miracle associated with Elisha occurred after his death. A dead man thrown into Elisha's tomb during a Moabite raid was restored to life.

With the change of kings in Syria, Jehoash was able to build up a stronger fighting force. Benhadad II was definitely placed in a defensive position as Jehoash regained much of the territory east of Jordan occupied by the Syrians under Hazael. Challenged by Amaziah of Judah, Jehoash defeated him, invaded Judah, broke down part of the Jerusalem wall, plundered the palace and the Temple, and took some hostages back to Samaria (ca. 791–790 B.C.).

Although Jehoash was disturbed over the loss of Elisha he was not sincerely interested in serving God but continued in his idolatrous ways. His short reign marked the turning point in the fortunes of Israel, as Elisha had predicted.

Jeroboam II, the fourth ruler in the Jehu dynasty, was the outstanding king in the Northern Kingdom. He reigned for forty-one years (793–753 B.C.), including a twelve-year coregency with his father. By the time he gained full control of the kingdom (781) he was in a position to take complete advantage of the opportunities for expansion.

Like that of Omri, the strongest king before him, the historiography of Jeroboam II is very brief in Scripture (2 Kings 14:23–29). The vast political and commercial expansion under this powerful king is summarized in the prophecy of Jonah, the son of Amittai, who may have been the prophet by that name sent on a mission to Nineveh (Jon. 1:1). Jonah predicted that Jeroboam would restore Israel from the Dead Sea to the borders of Hamath.

With Benhadad II, successor to Hazael at Damascus, in a weakened position, Jeroboam had the opportunity to recover the territory east of the Jordan that the Syrians had controlled for over a century. After 773 B.C. the Assyrian kings were so occupied with local and national problems that they did not threaten Palestine until after the time of Jeroboam. Consequently the Israelite kingdom enjoyed peaceful prosperity unequaled since the days of Solomon and David.

Samaria, which had been founded by Omri, now was refortified by Jeroboam. The wall was widened against the day of invasion to as much as thirty-three feet in some strategic places. The fortifications were so well built that about half a century later the Assyrians spent three years conquering the city.

Amos and Hosea, whose books appear in the Minor Prophets, reflect the prosperity of this period. The military and commercial success of Jeroboam brought an abundance of wealth to Israel. With this luxury came moral decline and religious indifference that these prophets boldly challenged. Jeroboam II had done evil in the sight of the Lord and caused Israel to sin, as Jeroboam the first king of the Northern Kingdom had done.

When Jeroboam II died in 753 B.C. he was succeeded by his son, Zechariah, whose reign lasted only six months. He was murdered by Shallum (2 Kings 15:8–12). This abruptly ended the long rule of the Jehu dynasty.

The Last Kings—2 Kings 15:13–17:41

The people who heard Amos and Hosea little realized how soon the threatened judgment would come upon Israel. In a period of only three decades (752–722 B.C.) the powerful Northern Kingdom ceased to exist as an independent nation. Under the expanding empire of Assyria it capitulated—never to rise again as an Israelite kingdom.

Menahem (752–741 B.C.) established himself successfully on the throne after Shallum's one-month rule was terminated by assassination. Menahem's most serious problem was Assyrian aggression. Coming to the Assyrian throne in 745 B.C., Tiglath-pileser III, or Pul, terrorized nations with his policy of taking captive leading citizens, executives, and political officials and replacing them with foreigners in conquered cities. In the years 743–738 B.C. Pul waged a northwestern campaign that involved a Palestinian coalition possibly led by Uzziah, king of Judah. In an Assyrian chronicle Menahem is cited as being re-enthroned on the condition that he pay tribute. This concession may have pacified Pul so that Menahem was relieved of Assyrian pressure, to die in peace.

Pekahiah followed the policies of his father. In continuing the collection of taxes as a vassal of Assyria, Pekahiah must have encountered opposition form his own people. Very likely Pekah championed a movement for revolt against Assyria and was responsible for the assassination of Pekahiah, which terminated his two-year reign.

Pekah's eight-year reign marked a period of both national and international crisis. Although Syria, with its capital of Damascus, may have been subjugated to Israel in the days of Jeroboam II, it asserted itself under the leadership of a new king, Rezin, during this period of Israel's decline. Since they faced a common foe in the Assyrians, Pekah strengthened his anti-Assyrian policy by collaboration with Rezin. While the Assyrians were primarily occupied with a campaign in Urartu (737–735 B.C.), these two kings endeavored to build a solid western alliance to resist Assyrian invasion.

In Judah the current pro-Assyrian party was successful (735 B.C.)

in bringing Ahaz into active control of the kingdom even though Jotham was still living. Consequently he resisted overtures from Israel and Syria to co-operate with them against Assyria. In 734 Pul invaded Philistia. Ahaz may have appealed to the Assyrians to relieve him from Philistine pressure (2 Chron. 28:16–21), or perhaps he already was a tributary of Pul. It may have been during this invasion that the Assyrians captured cities in the Northern Kingdom (2 Kings 15:29).

Syro-Israelite pressure on Judah ended in actual fighting known as the Syro-Ephraimitic War (2 Kings 16:5–9; 2 Chron. 28:5–15; Isa. 7:1–8:8). Syrian armies marched down to Elath to recover that seaport of Judah for the Edomites, who undoubtedly supported the coalition against Assyria. Although Jerusalem was besieged and captives from Judah were brought to Samaria and Damascus, the Southern Kingdom was neither subjugated nor coerced into this anti-Assyrian alliance.

Two important developments affected the withdrawal of the invading forces from Judah. When the captives were brought to Samaria a prophet, Oded by name, declared this to be divine judgment upon Judah and warned the Israelites of God's impending wrath. Owing to pressure from the princes and an Israelite assembly, the captives were released by the army officials.

The other important fact was that Ahaz refused to yield to the Syro-Ephraimitic demands but appealed directly to Pul for help. The Assyrian king had undoubtedly formulated his plans for subduing the westland. This invasion immediately stimulated him to action—Damascus becoming the focal point in the campaigns of 733 and 732 B.C. Pul boasts of taking 591 towns in this Syrian area, followed by the capitulation of Damascus in 732. Syria was rendered impotent, unable to interfere with the westward advance of Assyria. For the next century Damascus and its provinces—which for two hundred years had constituted the kingdom of Syria—were subject to Assyrian control.

The fall of Damascus had repercussions in Samaria. Pekah, who had come to power as the champion of an anti-Assyrian policy, now lost face. With Syria prostrate before Assyrian might, Israel's chances of survival were hopeless. Pekah became the victim of a conspiracy led by Hoshea, the next king. Undoubtedly it was the removal of Pekah that saved Samaria from conquest at this time.

As Hoshea became king of the Northern Kingdom in 731 B.C. he had little choice in his initial policy. He was a vassal of Tiglath-pileser III, who boasted of placing him on the throne in Samaria.

Hoshea's domain was largely confined to the hill country of Ephraim. Galilee and the territory east of the Jordan had been under Assyrian control since the campaign of 734. Pul may have conquered Megiddo during this series of western advances and used it as the administrative capital for his Galilean provinces.

In 727 B.C. Tiglath-pileser III, the great king of Assyria, died. Hoping that Shalmaneser V would not be able to maintain control of his extensive territory, Hoshea depended on the support of Egypt as he discontinued his payments of tribute to Assyria. Such, however, was not the case. Shalmaneser V marched his armies into Israel and besieged the strongly fortified city of Samaria in 725 B.C. For three years Hoshea was able to withstand the onslaught of the powerful Assyrian army, but he finally surrendered in 722 B.C.

This terminated the Northern Kingdom. Under the Assyrian policy of deportation, Israelites were taken into the regions of Persia. According to Assyrian annals, Sargon, Shalmaneser's successor, claimed nearly twenty-eight thousand victims. In return, colonists from Babylonia were settled in Samaria—the Northern Kingdom was reduced to the status of an Assyrian province.

For two centuries the Israelites had followed the pattern set by Jeroboam I, founder of the Northern Kingdom. Even with the change of dynasties, Israel never divorced itself from the idolatry that was diametrically opposed to the law of God as prescribed in the Decalogue. Throughout this period faithful prophets proclaimed God's message, warning the kings as well as the people of impending judgment. For their gross idolatry and failure to serve God, the Israelites were subjected to captivity at the hands of the Assyrian rulers.

Chapter 9

THE SOUTHERN KINGDOM

The disruption of the Solomonic kingdom left the Davidic dynasty with only a small segment of its former empire. With Jerusalem as its capital the royal line of David maintained the kingdom of Judah until its conquest by the Babylonians in 586 B.C.

Rehoboam—1 Kings 12:1-24; 2 Chronicles 10:1-12:16

As successor to his father's throne Rehoboam faced rebellion upon Solomon's death. The immediate cause of the rebellion of the northern tribes, led by the tribe of Ephraim, was his taxation policy. Egypt may have had a vital part in this disruption since Jeroboam, the first king of the Northern Kingdom, found refuge in Egypt when fleeing from Solomon. Explicitly mentioned in the biblical account is that this rebellion was a divine judgment for Solomon's apostasy and idolatry—postponed until after the death of Solomon.

Real religious fervor was promoted throughout Judah during the first three years after this political division, as priests and Levites left the Northern Kingdom because of Jeroboam's substitution of idolatry for true religion. Although Rehoboam began his reign with sincere religious devotion, he apostatized, but only after he had succeeded in establishing his kingdom by fortifying many cities throughout Judah. When Shishak of Egypt invaded Judah, a prophet named Shemaiah announced that this was a divine judgment but that Judah would not be destroyed.

Rehoboam's seventeen-year reign was generally a time of turmoil as war continued between the North and the South. Following the example set by his father, he succumbed to idolatry and practiced polygamy.

Abijah—1 Kings 15:1–8; 2 Chronicles 13:1–22

During his three-year reign Abijah activated the chronic warfare between Judah and Israel by aggressively challenging Jeroboam within Ephraimite territory. By continuing in the tradition of religious inclusivism begun by Solomon and promoted by Rehoboam, he made idolatry stronger and more widespread throughout his kingdom.

Asa—1 Kings 15:9–24; 2 Chronicles 14:1–16:14

Peaceful conditions prevailed during the first decade of Asa's long reign (910–869 B.C.) In spite of his youth and the influence of Maacah, who continued as queen mother, Asa began a program of reform and admonished the people to keep the Mosaic law. After repulsing an attack by an Ethiopian army and achieving victory through divine aid, Asa was encouraged by the prophet Azariah to activate his reform program throughout his kingdom.

Encouraged by the prophet and the king, the people entered into a covenant to serve God wholeheartedly as they repaired the altar of the Lord. Undoubtedly it was with this public support that Asa removed Maacah as queen mother. Religious celebrations, greater than any held since the Solomonic dedication of the Temple, attracted many Israelites from the Northern Kingdom to Jerusalem. Fearing defection of his people to Jerusalem, Baasha, who had just seized the throne in Israel, began to fortify the city of Ramah, located five miles north where the roads leading to Jerusalem converged. Asa allied himself with the Syrian king, Benhadad, and the armies of Syria seized territory and cities in northern Israel, causing Baasha to withdraw his armies from Ramah.

Asa was rebuked for his ungodly affiliation with Benhadad by the prophet Hanani, who warned him that he would be subjected to wars because he had ignored God in this crisis. Angered by this rebuke, Asa imprisoned Hanani. Nothing is recorded about the rest of his reign. Two years prior to his death Asa was stricken by a fatal disease.

Jehoshaphat—1 Kings 22:41–50; 2 Chronicles 17:1–20:37

In the early years of his 25-year reign (872–848 B.C.) Jehoshaphat revived the policies of religious reform that had been so effective in the first part of Asa's reign. This renewed interest in God had a wholesome effect upon the surrounding nations as well as upon Judah. As Jehoshaphat fortified his cities and received tribute and acclaim from the Philistines and Arabs, he prospered politically as well as religiously.

Friendship between Judah and Israel was established in the marriage alliance between the Davidic and Omride dynasties in the first decade of Jehoshaphat's reign. This bond, sealed by the marriage of his son Jehoram to Athaliah, the daughter of Ahab and Jezebel, insured Jehoshaphat against attack and invasion from the north. In 853 B.C. he joined Ahab and other Palestinian forces in the battle of Karkar, resisting the westward aggression of the Assyrians. Later that year Jehoshaphat joined Ahab in his attempt to recover Ramoth Gilead and narrowly escaped with his life. Ahab was killed in battle.

Returning to Jerusalem, Jehoshaphat was severely rebuked by the prophet Jehu for his ungodly alliance with Ahab. Responding favorably to this solemn warning, he personally encouraged his people to turn to God. He implemented his reform by appointing judges with the admonition that they should judge righteously without showing partiality or accepting bribes.

When Jehoshaphat was confronted with a terrible invasion from the southeast, he proclaimed a fast, led his people in prayer, and appealed to God for deliverance. He admonished them to exercise faith in God and in the prophets as they chanted praises to God in their march against the enemy. After a miraculous victory the fear of God fell on the nations round about.

Jehoshaphat continued his close affinity with the wicked Omride dynasty. In a joint naval venture at Ezion-geber for commercial purposes, the ships were wrecked as predicted by Eliezer the prophet. Later Jehoshaphat joined Joram, another son of Ahab, in marching through Edom to subdue Moab. On this occasion he was made conscious of his ungodly alliance by the prophet Elisha. Although this policy of intermarriage with the Omride dynasty did not seriously affect his nation as long as he lived, it almost eliminated the Davidic dynasty from Judah less than a decade after his death. The fruition of his inclusivist policy largely nullified the lifetime efforts of godly Jehoshaphat.

Jehoram—2 Kings 8:16–24; 2 Chronicles 21:1–20

Although Jehoram was coregent with his father, he did not assume much responsibility until after Jehoshaphat's death. He soon replaced his father's peaceful rule with bloodshed and idolatry. He murdered his six brothers, killed princes, and espoused the sinful ways of Ahab and Jezebel, very likely influenced by his wife, Athaliah.

Jehoram was severely reproached in writing by Elijah the prophet. He was warned of impending judgment for his crime in killing his brothers and leading Judah into the sinful ways of the Northern Kingdom. The gloomy future held a plague for Judah and an incurable disease for the king himself.

Edom revolted and gained independence. The Philistines and Arabs not only revolted but advanced into Jerusalem, even raiding the king's house and taking captive Jehoram's family, sparing only his wife, Athaliah, and her son, Ahaziah. Jehoram was stricken with a fatal disease two years before his death, and after terrible suffering he died in 841 B.C. No one regretted his death; he was not even accorded the usual honor of being buried in the tombs of the kings.

Ahaziah—2 Kings 8:25-29; 2 Chronicles 22:1-9

Ahaziah had the shortest reign during this period, less than a year (841 B.C.). Since all of Jehoram's other sons had been killed by the Arabs, the people of Judah had no choice but to crown Ahaziah king. With the pattern set by his father, Ahaziah had little choice himself. Under the influence of his mother, Athaliah, and his uncle, Joram, who ruled in Samaria, the wickedness of Ahab and Jezebel found full expression in the kingdom of Judah.

Ahaziah joined the Israelites in battle against Syria. He was in Jezreel, the summer palace of the Omride dynasty, where Joram was recovering from wounds received on the battlefront, when the revolution erupted in Israel. Jehu marched on Jezreel, mortally wounding Joram. Escaping from Jezreel, Ahaziah himself was fatally wounded and died in Megiddo. As a mark of respect for Jehoshaphat, this grandson, Ahaziah, was given a royal burial.

Athaliah—2 Kings 11:1-21; 2 Chronicles 22:10-23:21

In a reign of terror Athaliah occupied the Davidic throne in Jerusalem for six years (841-835 B.C.). Seizing control after the burial of her son Ahaziah, she ordered the execution of everyone of royal descent. Apparently only Joash, the infant son of Ahaziah, escaped, under the care of Jehosheba. She appropriated the dedicated objects in the Temple for Baal worship and made Mattan the high priest of Baal in Jerusalem. In the seventh year of her reign, Jehoiada, a priest who had witnessed the religious revivals under Asa and Jehoshaphat, secured the support of the palace guards, crowned Joash king, and ordered the arrest and execution of Athaliah.

Joash—2 Kings 12:1-21; 2 Chronicles 24:1-27

With a seven-year-old king on the throne, the state policies were formulated and directed by Jehoiada. The altars of Baal were broken down, and Mattan was killed. Jehoiada initiated a covenant in which the people promised to serve God. In time the Temple, which had been neglected since Jehoshaphat's time, was restored as interest prevailed in true worship. Popular support of the true religion reached a new peak under Jehoiada's influence.

After the death of Jehoiada, apostasy swept in as the princes of Judah persuaded Joash to revert to idols and the asherim service. When Zechariah, the son of Jehoiada, warned the people that they would not prosper if they continued to disobey the commandments of the Lord, he was stoned in the court of the Temple. Joash did not even remember the kindness of Jehoiada by saving the life of Zechariah.

Judgment came upon Judah; they were threatened with invasion by the Syrians under King Hazael, who already had extended his kingdom southward at the expense of the Northern Kingdom. After his conquest of Gath on the Philistine plain, he set his face toward Jerusalem. Joash avoided invasion by sending Temple treasures and palace gold to appease Hazael. Presumably it was the failure to pay further tribute that impelled the Aramaean king to send a contingent of troops against Jerusalem some time later. After killing some of the princes and leaving Joash wounded, they returned to Damascus with the spoils. The palace servants took advantage of the situation to avenge the blood of Zechariah by assassinating their king. Joash was buried in the city of David but not in the tombs of the kings.

Amaziah—2 Kings 14:1–22; 2 Chronicles 25:1–28

With the abrupt termination of the reign of Joash, Amaziah was immediately crowned king of Judah. Although he reigned a total of twenty-nine years (796–767 B.C.) he was sole ruler for only a short period. After 791 B.C. Uzziah, his son, began to reign as coregent on the Davidic throne.

Both Judah and Israel had suffered seriously under the aggressive power of Hazael, king of Syria. His death at the turn of the century marked the turning point in the fortunes of the Hebrew kingdoms.

Jehoash, who ascended the throne of Israel in Samaria in 798 B.C., developed a strong army that in time challenged Syrian might. Amaziah adopted a similar policy for Judah, which enabled his nation to recuperate from invasion and royal bloodshed.

One of Amaziah's first aggressive acts was to defeat Edom with his own army and capture Seir. Instead of acknowledging God in this victory, he introduced the Edomite gods to his people in Jerusalem and worshiped those gods. With a victory over Edom to his credit he was so confident of his military might that he challenged Jehoash, the king of Israel, to a battle. Warned by a prophet that he would fail, Amaziah attacked Israel nevertheless and was utterly defeated. The victors broke down part of the wall of Jerusalem, plundered the city, and took Amaziah captive. With royal hostages and much spoil Jehoash returned jubilantly to Samaria. How disastrous this defeat was for Amaziah is not fully stated in the Scriptures. The act of breaching the wall meant total subjugation in the language of the ancient world.

With the capture of Amaziah (ca. 791–790 B.C.), the leaders of Judah made sixteen-year-old Uzziah coregent with his father, who was held prisoner as long as Jehoash lived. When the latter died (ca. 781–782 B.C.), Jeroboam, who had been coregent since 793 B.C., assumed full command of the expanding Northern Kingdom. The release of Amaziah may have been part of his goodwill policy toward Judah as he directed his effort toward regaining the territory that had been lost to Syria.

Although Amaziah had bright hopes for retrieving the fortunes of Judah at the beginning of his reign, his prospects for success were shattered with his capture by Jehoash. When he was restored to the Davidic throne in Jerusalem in either 782 or 781 B.C., he must have been quite ineffective in leading his nation back to a position of supremacy. Throughout the rest of his reign Judah was overshadowed by Israelite expansion. Amaziah finally fled to Lachish, where he fell victim to pursuing assassins.

Uzziah (Azariah)—2 Kings 15:1-7; 2 Chronicles 16:1-23

Outstanding in Judah's history is the reign of Uzziah (791-740 B.C.). Even though crucial events occurred during his 52-year rule, the biblical account is relatively brief. Noteworthy is that during this long period Uzziah was sole ruler for only seventeen years. So effective was he in lifting Judah from vassalage to a strong national power that he is recognized as the most able sovereign the Sothern Kingdom had known since Solomon.

When Uzziah was suddenly elevated to kingship the national hopes of Judah had sunk to the lowest point since the division of the Solomonic kingdom. The defeat at the hands of Israel was nothing less than a calamity. When Amaziah gained his freedom it is doubtful that he had the respect of his people; the whole nation was suffering the consequences of his disastrous policy. Very likely Uzziah continued to wield considerable influence in affairs of state. Judah's vassalage to Israel must have terminated, at the latest, with Amaziah's death or perhaps with his release fifteen years earlier. A policy of friendliness and co-operation very likely prevailed between Uzziah and Jeroboam II.

Uzziah restored the walls of Jerusalem, improved fortifications around the capital city, and organized and equipped the army with superlative weapons. To the southwest he defeated the Philistines and the Arabs. To the south he extended the borders of Judah to Elath on the Gulf of Aqaba. Eastward he collected tribute from the Ammonites and may have extended his control over the Transjordan area after the death of Jeroboam.

By promoting agriculture and animal husbandry he improved Judah economically. Large herds in desert areas necessitated the digging of wells and the erection of towers for protection. Vinedressers expanded their production. Territorial expansion placed Judah in control of important commercial cities and highways leading into Arabia, Egypt, and other countries. At Elath on the Red Sea, the copper and mining industries, which flourished under David and

Solomon, were reclaimed for Judah. Although Judah lagged behind the Northern Kingdom in its military and economic expansion, it enjoyed a steady growth under Uzziah's leadership and continued its prosperity even when Israel began to decline after Jeroboam's death. Judah's growth and influence during this period were second only to that experienced in the days of David and Solomon.

Uzziah's prosperity was directly related to his dependence upon God. Zechariah, a prophet otherwise unknown, effectively instructed the king, who, until about 750 B.C., had a wholesome and humble attitude toward God. At the height of his success, however, Uzziah assumed that he could enter the Temple and burn incense. With the support of eighty priests, the high priest, whose name was also Azariah, confronted Uzziah with the fact that this was the prerogative of those consecrated for this purpose (Exod. 30:7; Num. 18:1-7). In anger the king defied the priests. As a result of divine judgment, Uzziah became leprous. For the rest of his reign he was ostracized from the palace and denied the ordinary social privileges. He could not even enter the Temple. Jotham was made coruler and assumed the royal responsibilities for the remainder of his father's life.

The ominous threat of Assyrian aggression also dampened the national hopes of Judah during the last decade of Uzziah's long and successful reign. If he had hopes of restoring the whole Solomonic empire to Judah after the death of Jeroboam II, Uzziah saw them shattered by rising Assyrian power. In 745 B.C. Tiglath-pileser III began to carve out his empire. He subdued Babylon and then turned westward to defeat Sarduris III, king of Urartu. During his northwestern campaign (743-738 B.C.) he encountered opposition as he moved into Syria. In his annals he mentions fighting against Azariah, king of Judah, at the beginning of this campaign (ca. 743). Although Tiglath-pileser crushed the opposition led by Azariah, he made no claim to collecting tribute from Judah. Since Menaham had paid an enormous sum to avoid a punitive invasion by the ferocious Assyrians, Tiglath-pileser did not advance his armies southward to Judah at this time. Uzziah was able, therefore, to maintain an anti-Assyrian policy with pro-Assyrian Israel as a buffer state to the north.

Jotham—2 Kings 15:32-38; 2 Chronicles 27:1-9

As coregent Jotham had a secondary position as long as his father, who was a strong and forceful ruler, lived. Upon Uzziah's death in 740 B.C. Jotham assumed sole control, attempting to continue the same domestic and economic policies. He subdued a revolt of the Ammonites and continued to collect tribute from them for the first three years of his reign.

With an ominous Assyrian invasion pending, Jotham faced trouble in maintaining his anti-Assyrian policy. When the Assyrian armies became active in the regions of Mount Nal and Urartu in 736-735, a pro-Assyrian party in Jerusalem elevated Ahaz to the Davidic throne as coregent with Jotham. Assyrian records confirm 735 as the date for the accession of Ahaz. Jotham died in 732.

Ahaz—2 Kings 16:1-20; 2 Chronicles 28:1-27

Ahaz, made king at the age of twenty, faced serious international problems with Israel, Syria, and Assyria. Under Pekah, the Northern Kingdom, allied with Syria, had adopted a policy of resistance toward Assyria. Ahaz may have appealed to the Assyrian king to aid him in resisting Philistine raids on Judah's outlying districts. When the Assyrian armies withdrew, Pekah, king of Israel, and Rezin, king of Syria, declared war on Judah.

At the time of this distressing crisis Isaiah had been active in the prophetic ministry for about six years. With a message from God, he confronted Ahaz with the solution to his problem. Faith in God was the key to victory over Israel and Syria. Pekah and Rezin intended to place a puppet ruler on the Davidic throne in Jerusalem, but God would nullify the Syro-Ephraimitic scheme in response to faith (Isa. 7:1 ff.). The stubbornly wicked Ahaz ignored Isaiah. In defiance, he sought a way out of his difficulty by making a desperate appeal to Tiglath-pileser III.

When the armies of Syria and Israel invaded Judah they besieged but could not take Jerusalem, which had so recently been refortified by Uzziah. Though hard pressed, Ahaz survived the Syro-Ephraimitic attack. As a result of his appeal to Tiglath-pileser the Assyrians subsequently advanced to conquer Damascus in 732 B.C., bringing that kingdom to an end. There Ahaz met the Assyrian king and assured him of Judah's vassalage. Duplicating the Damascus altar in the Temple in Jerusalem, Ahaz promoted pagan worship and brought condemnation upon his own head.

Throughout his reign Ahaz maintained a pro-Assyrian policy. As rulers changed in Assyria and the Northern Kingdom came to an end with Hoshea's rebellion, Ahaz successfully guided his nation through these international crises, paying tribute to Assyria. However, he incurred God's wrath by promoting the most obnoxious idolatrous practices and introducing foreign cults into the very place where God alone was to be worshiped.

Hezekiah—2 Kings 18:1–20:21; 2 Chronicles 29:1–32:33; Isaiah 36–39

Hezekiah's 29-year reign (716–686 B.C.) marks an outstanding religious era in the history of Judah. Although beleaguered by the Assyrians, he survived the crucial attack on Jerusalem in 701.

In drastic reaction to the deliberate idolatry of his father, Hezekiah began his reign with the most extensive reform in the history of Judah. As a young man of twenty-five he had witnessed the gradual disintegration of the Northern Kingdom and the Assyrian conquest of Samaria, only forty miles north of Jerusalem. With the keen realization that Israel's captivity was the consequence of a broken covenant and disobedience to God, Hezekiah placed his confidence in the God of Israel. During the early years of his reign he led an effective reform, not only in Judah but also in parts of Israel. Since Judah already was a vassal of Assyria, Hezekiah acknowledged the suzerainty of Sargon II (721–705 B.C.). Although Assyrian troops were dispatched to Ashdod in 711 B.C., the king of Judah had no serious interference from Assyria.

The Temple was reopened, repaired, and cleansed by the Levites and ready for worship in sixteen days. Musical groups, with their harps, cymbals, and lyres, accompanied the singers who praised God in the words of David and Asaph while the officials brought their sacrifices. Letters were sent throughout Israel as well as Judah inviting the Israelites to come to Jerusalem for the Passover. Many responded and joined in this celebration, which exceeded all festal observances since the dedication of the Temple.

With the death of Sargon II (705) revolutions broke out in many parts of the Assyrian empire. By 702 Merodach-baladan was quelled, removed from the Babylonian throne, and replaced by Bel-ibni, a native Chaldean who probably was a member of the royal family. In Egypt nationalism surged forward under the energetic leadership of Shabako, an Ethiopian king, who founded the Twenty-fifth Dynasty about 710 B.C. With other nations in the Fertile Crescent rebelling against him, Sennacherib, son of Sargon, turned his armies westward. After subduing Phoenicia and other coastal resistance, the Assyrian armies successfully occupied the Philistine area in 701 B.C.

In anticipation of this Assyrian attack Hezekiah had reinforced fortifications around Jerusalem and constructed a 1,777-foot tunnel from the spring of Gihon to the Siloam pool to ensure an adequate water supply. Having done all he could to prepare militarily, Hezekiah assembled his people at the city square and boldly expressed his confidence in God, "With him is only the arm of flesh, but with us is the Lord our God to help us and to fight our battles."

Sennacherib's threat became a reality in 701 B.C. Conquering Sidon, Joppa, and other cities en route, the Assyrians conquered Ekron and defeated the Egyptians at Eltekeh. Hezekiah not only was forced to release Padi, the king of Ekron, whom he had taken captive, but also paid a heavy tribute, stripping the Temple of its silver and gold.

Most likely it was during this period of Assyrian pressure, about 701 B.C., that Hezekiah became seriously ill. Although Isaiah warned the king to prepare for death, God intervened. Twofold was the divine promise to the king of Judah—a fifteen-year extension of his life and deliverance of Jerusalem from the Assyrian threat.

Claiming that he was God-commissioned, Sennacherib sent his officers to Jerusalem demanding capitulation and surrender, but when they heard rumors of a Babylonian revolt, the Assyrians abandoned their siege of Libnah and departed immediately. Even though Sennacherib had conquered forty-six walled cities belonging to Hezekiah, he makes no such claim for Jerusalem. He boasted in his annals of some two hundred thousand Judean captives and reported that Hezekiah was shut up in Jerusalem like a caged bird.

Acclaim and recognition was expressed by the surrounding nations in abundant gifts to Hezekiah following his successful resistance to the Assyrians and his physical recovery. The Babylonian embassy very likely was duly impressed with the display of wealth in Jerusalem. Hezekiah's triumph, however, was tempered by the subsequent warning of Isaiah that succeeding generations would be subjected to Babylonian captivity. Nevertheless this outstanding deliverance may have given the religious reformation a new impetus while peace and prosperity prevailed during the extended reign of Hezekiah.

In the Tigris-Euphrates area the Assyrian king suppressed rebellions and in 689 B.C. destroyed the city of Babylon. Proceeding successfully into Arabia Sennacherib heard of the advance of Tirhakah. Since Egypt may have been the real objective of the Assyrian campaign in 701 B.C., it may well be that Sennacherib now hoped to ward off Judean interference by dispatching letters to Hezekiah with an ultimatum of surrender. With letters in hand, Hezekiah went to the Temple to pray. Through Isaiah he was assured that the Assyrian king would return by the way he came. Just where the army was encamped when it incurred the loss of 185,000 troops is not indicated in the scriptural records, but apparently it never reached Jerusalem. Hezekiah continued to reign in peace until he died in 686 B.C. He was buried with honor.

Manasseh—2 Kings 21:1-18; 2 Chronicles 33:1-20

Including the decade of coregency with his father, Manasseh had the longest reign in the history of Judah (696–942 B.C.). In character and practice he resembled his grandfather Ahaz, and he catapulted Judah into its darkest era of idolatry.

By rebuilding the high places, erecting altars to Baal, and constructing asherim, Manasseh plunged Judah into gross idolatry like that which Ahab and Jezebel had promoted in the Northern Kingdom. Through religious rites and ceremonies, worship of stars and planets was instituted. Even the Ammonite deity Molech was acknowledged by the Hebrew king in the sacrifice of children in the Hinnom valley, outside Jerusalem. Human sacrifice was one of the most abominable rites of Canaanitic paganism and was associated by the psalmist with demon worship (106:36-37). Astrology, divination, and occultism were officially sanctioned and became common practices. In open defiance of God, altars for worshiping the host of heaven were placed in the courts of the Temple, while graven images of Asherah, the wife of Baal, were placed in the Temple itself. In addition, Manasseh shed much innocent blood; possibly he was responsible for the martyrdom of Isaiah. The moral and religious conditions in Judah were worse than those of the nations that had been exterminated or expelled from Canaan. Manasseh thus represented the low point of wickedness in the long list of Davidic kings. The judgments predicted by Isaiah were sure to come.

Manasseh curried the favor of Assyria in subservient vassalage while Esarhaddon (681–669 B.C.) extended his control down into Egypt. In contrast to Sennacherib, Esarhaddon adopted a conciliatory policy and rebuilt the city of Babylon. He subjugated Tyre in 678, occupied Memphis in 673, and a few years later captured Tirhakah. In his list of twenty-two kings from the Hittite country, he mentions Manasseh, king of Judah, among those who made a compulsory visit to Nineveh in 678 B.C. Although Babylon had been rebuilt by that time, it is not at all certain that Manasseh was taken there by Esarhaddon.

With the destruction of Thebes in 663 B.C., Ashurbanipal, who began his reign in 669, extended Assyrian control five hundred miles along the Nile into Upper Egypt. A bloody civil war shook the Assyrian empire (652) in the rebellion of Shamash-shum-ukin, who was a brother of Ashurbanipal and vassal king of Babylon. By the time this insurrection climaxed in the conquest of Babylon in 648, rebellions had erupted in Syria and Palestine. Judah may have participated by joining Edom and Moab, who are named in the Assyrian inscriptions. Moab's autonomy was terminated at this time, and Judah's king, Manasseh, was taken captive to Babylon but subsequently released.

Manasseh may have been captured in 648 B.C. and possibly returned to Jerusalem as vassal king in the same year. If so, then he had relatively little time left to undo the religious practices he had fostered for so many years. Having repented in captivity, he now exemplified the fear of God in commanding the people to serve God. It is doubtful that his reform was very effective, since those who had served under Hezekiah in true worship had previously been removed or executed.

Amon—2 Kings 21:19-26; 2 Chronicles 33:21-25

Without hesitation Amon reverted to the idolatrous practices that had been initiated and promoted by Manasseh during the major part of his kingship. Although he was slain by his palace slaves in 642 B.C., Amon set a godless example during his two-year reign that provided the opportunity for Judah to revert to a terrible state of apostasy.

Josiah—2 Kings 22:1-23:30; 2 Chronicles 34:1-35:27

At the early age of eight Josiah was suddenly crowned king to begin a 31-year reign (640-609 B.C.). The kingdom of Judah had for a century survived the successful expansion of the Assyrian empire. Ever since Ahaz had forfeited Judah's freedom in a treaty with Tiglath-pileser III, this little kingdom had weathered crisis after crisis as a vassal to five more Assyrian rulers. Treaties, diplomatic maneuvers, resistance, and supernatural intervention all had a vital bearing on the continuous existence of a semiautonomous government as a succession of wicked, then righteous, kings occupied the Davidic throne. Assyria was relaxing its clutch on Judah, and nationalistic hopes rose once more during the three decades of Josiah's reign. However, the abrupt termination of Josiah's leadership marked the beginning of the end for the Southern Kingdom. Under the rising power of the Babylonian empire the kingdom of Judah was terminated with the destruction of Jerusalem in 586 B.C.

The declining influence of Assyria in the closing years of Ashurbanipal, who died about 630 B.C., had afforded Judah the opportunity to extend its influence over the territory northward, perhaps sparking in Judah's political leaders the hope of including the northern tribes and even the boundaries of the Solomonic kingdom in the Southern Kingdom. With the fall of the Assyrian city of Ashur to the Medes in 614, and the destruction of Nineveh in 612 by the allied forces of Media and Babylonia, Judah's prospects had been even more favorable. During this period of political unrest and rebellion in the east, Judah gained complete freedom from Assyrian vassalage, which naturally gave rise to nationalism.

With idolatry permeating the kingdom, the religious prospects for the boy-king were anything but hopeful. As Josiah grew to manhood he reacted against the sinful conditions of his time. At the age of sixteen he was earnestly taking God into account rather than conforming to idolatrous practices. During the next four years his devotion to God crystallized to the point that he began a religious reformation (628 B.C.). In the eighteenth year of his reign (622), while the Temple was being repaired, "the book of the Law of the Lord that had been given through Moses" was discovered by the priest Hilkiah. After hearing it read by Huldah, the prophetess, Josiah led his people in observing the Passover.

By this time it was politically safe for Josiah to remove any religious practices that were associated with Judah's vassalage to Assyria. Asserting his kingly authority, he took drastic measures to rid his kingdom of idolatry. Altars of Baal were broken down; asherim were destroyed; chambers of cult prostitution in the Temple were renovated, and horses dedicated to the sun were removed from the Temple's entrance, and the chariots destroyed by fire. The horrible practice of child sacrifice was abruptly abolished. The altars erected by Manasseh in the court of the Temple were crushed and the pieces scattered in the Kidron valley. Even some of the high places erected by Solomon must have been in current use, since Josiah razed them and desecrated them with human bones. Priests dedicated to idol worship were removed from office. At Bethel the altar that had been erected by Jeroboam I was destroyed under Josiah's orders (cf. 1 Kings 13). Throughout the cities of Samaria, high places were removed and priests were arrested for their idolatrous ministry.

Under the king's leadership the elders of Judah, priests and Levites, and the populace of Jerusalem assembled for public reading of the newly found book. In a solemn covenant King Josiah, supported by the people, promised that he would devote himself wholly to obedience to the law.

Whether the reformation under Josiah represented a genuine revival among the common people is doubtful. Since it was initiated and executed under royal orders, the opposition was restrained as long as Josiah lived. Immediately after his death the people reverted to idolatry under Jehoiakim.

Jeremiah was called to the prophetic ministry in the thirteenth year of Josiah's reign, 627 B.C. Since Josiah had already begun his reform, it is reasonable to conclude that prophet and king worked hand in hand. When the book of the law was read, the king's urgent need for an immediate solution to his problem may have made it necessary to involve Huldah, who resided in Jerusalem, instead of Jeremiah, who lived in Anathoth, three miles northeast of the city.

As the news of the fall of Ashur (614) and the destruction of Nineveh (612) was circulated in Jerusalem, Josiah undoubtedly turned his attention to international affairs. In a state of military preparedness, he made his fatal mistake. In 609 the Assyrians were fighting a losing battle with their government in exile at Haran. Necho, king of Egypt, marched his armies through Palestine to aid the Assyrians. Since Josiah had little concern for the preservation of the Assyrians, he rushed his armies up to Megiddo in an effort to stop the Egyptians. Josiah was fatally wounded when his armies were routed. Suddenly the national and religious hopes of Judah vanished as the 39-year-old king was entombed in the city of David. After eighteen years of intimate association with Josiah, the great prophet Jeremiah is singled out by name in the concluding paragraph of the biblical account: "Jeremiah composed laments for Josiah."

Jehoahaz (Shallum)—2 Kings 23:31–34; 2 Chronicles 36:1–4

The people of Judah enthroned Jehoahaz in Jerusalem. Necho marched his army north to Carchemish, temporarily halting the westward advance of the Babylonians. Establishing his headquarters at Riblah, Necho deposed Jehoahaz as king of Judah and took him as prisoner to Egypt, ending a three-month reign.

Jehoiakim (Eliakim)—2 Kings 23:35–24:7; 2 Chronicles 36:5–8

Eliakim, another son of Josiah, had his name changed to Jehoiakim when he was enthroned by Necho, to whom he paid heavy tribute as he began his eleven-year reign (609–598 B.C.).

Jeremiah faced severe opposition with Jehoiakim as king. Predicting Babylonian captivity and the destruction of the Temple (Jer. 26), Jeremiah was subjected to mob violence, but his life was spared through Ahikam, a prominent political figure in Jerusalem. In the fourth year of his reign Jehoiakim had Jeremiah's scroll read before him and then threw it into the fire, ignoring this divine warning (Jer. 36).

In 605 B.C. the Babylonian armies under Nebuchadnezzar defeated the Egyptians at Carchemish in a decisive battle. Advancing into Palestine, Nebuchadnezzar claimed treasures and hostages in Jerusalem, including Daniel and his friends (Dan. 1:1). Although Jehoiakim retained his throne, he became a vassal of Nebuchadnezzar, who was enthroned in Babylon that same year. When Jehoiakim rebelled, the Babylonian armies advanced toward Jerusalem in 598. Jehoiakim's reign was abruptly terminated by death, however, three months before their arrival. Very likely he died in warfare with maurauding Chaldean bands, since his body was cast out beyond the gates of Jerusalem as Jeremiah had predicted (cf. Jer. 22:18–19; 36:27–32).

Jehoiachin (Jeconiah)—2 Kings 24:8–17; 2 Chronicles 36:9–10

Jehoiachin, son of Jehoiakim, lasted only three months as king in Jerusalem. In 597 the Babylonian armies surrounded the city, and Jehoiachin surrendered to Nebuchadnezzar. Besides stripping the Temple and the royal treasuries, the king took Jehoiachin and his queen mother, palace officials, executives, artisans, and all leaders in the community into captivity in Babylon. Not least among these thousands was Ezekiel. Mattaniah, whose name Nebuchadnezzar changed to Zedekiah, was left in charge of the people who remained in Jerusalem.

Zedekiah (Mattaniah)—2 Kings 24:18–25:7; 2 Chronicles 36:11–21

Zedekiah, the youngest son of Josiah, was regarded as a puppet king. After a decade of weak and vacillating policies, he forfeited the national government of Judah.

Jeremiah continued his ministry with the lower-class people left in Jerusalem. He wrote letters to the exiles in Babylon encouraging them to adjust themselves to exilic conditions since they could not expect to return to Judah for seventy years (Jer. 25:11–12; 29:10). He warned Zedekiah not to yield to pressure to join the Egyptians in rebelling against the Babylonians. False prophets opposed Jeremiah, making it very difficult for him.

In 588 Zedekiah joined in a plan of rebellion that resulted in the siege of Jerusalem by the Babylonian armies. During this siege Jeremiah advised him to surrender, but he cast his lot with the leaders who were determined to hold out to the bitter end.

In the summer of 586 the Babylonians captured the city, blinded Zedekiah, and took him in chains to Babylon. The great Solomonic Temple, which had been the pride and glory of Israel for four centuries, was reduced to ashes, and the city of Jerusalem lay in ruins.

For additional study help see *Figure 9* in the Appendix.

Chapter 10

RETURN FROM BABYLON

The Neo-Babylonian kingdom gained international supremacy under Nabopolassar (626–605 B.C.) and his son Nebuchadnezzar (605–562 B.C.). The latter terminated the Davidic kingdom by destroying Jerusalem with its temple in 586 B.C., sending the Jews into exile

Exile in Babylonia

The new home of the Jews was Babylonia in the lower Euphrates valley. The city of Babylon was a strategic commercial and religious center in the Assyrian empire as it dominated the Fertile Crescent for over a century, beginning in 745 B.C. With the death of Ashurbanipal (ca. 633 B.C.), Nabopolassar emerged as the political leader who continued to champion the cause of Babylonian independence, successfully establishing himself as king of Babylon on November 22–23, 626 B.C. As a result of a Medo-Babylonian alliance, which was confirmed by marriage, Nineveh was destroyed in 612 B.C. By 609 B.C. the Babylonians had routed the last vestige of the Assyrian armies from Haran and established control of the upper Euphrates area.

In early summer, 605 B.C., Nebuchadnezzar led the Babylonian armies to a decisive victory over the Egyptians at Carchemish and advanced their control over Judah, exacting tribute and royal hostages, including Daniel, from Jehoiakim in Jerusalem. As crown prince, Nebuchadnezzar immediately rushed back to Babylon when news reached him of the death of his father on August 15–16. On

September 6–7 he was crowned king of Babylon. Subsequently the Egyptians were decisively routed from Palestine as Nebuchadnezzar took Jehoiachin and thousands of Jews captive in 597 B.C. and ultimately denuded Jerusalem of its population, leaving it in ruins in 586 B.C. and terminating the Davidic kingdom. In subsequent decades Egypt yielded to Babylonian control.

Nebuchadnezzar devoted intensive efforts during his long reign to building projects throughout Babylonia. The city of Babylon was fortified by a moat and a double wall. Throughout the city a vast system of streets and canals was built to facilitate transportation. Along the broad processional street and in the palace were lions, bulls, and dragons made of colored enamel bricks. The noted Ishtar Gate marked the impressive entrance into this street. Bricks used in ordinary construction bore the imprint of Nebuchadnezzar's own name. Some twenty temples in Babylon and Borsippa are credited to this famous king, but the most outstanding was the reconstruction of the ziggurat. The hanging gardens, built by Nebuchadnezzar to please his Median queen, were regarded by the Greeks as one of the seven wonders of the world. Nebuchadnezzar's arrogant boast that he built this great city by his might and for his glory is recognized as historically accurate (Dan. 4:30).

Daniel, taken as a hostage to the royal court in Babylon in 605 B.C., was recognized with his friends as far superior to all other wise men "in every matter of wisdom and understanding" (Dan. 1:17–21). Faced with the threat of execution, Daniel appealed to Nebuchadnezzar for time to respond to the king's demand to tell him his dream. After prayer with his friends Daniel not only related in detail the king's dream but also gave him its interpretation. Immediately Daniel was made ruler over the province of Babylon and given the highest position among all wise men in the king's court (2:1–49).

Through another dream Nebuchadnezzar was warned that he would be humiliated if he did not renounce his sin. A year later, boasting about building Babylon as his royal residence by "my mighty power and the glory of my majesty," Nebuchadnezzar was suddenly smitten with lycanthropy in divine judgment. After living with the beasts of the fields for several years his reason was restored to him. In a public proclamation Nebuchadnezzar acknowledged God as the "Most High" and the "King of heaven" who rules over all the earth (4:1–37).

Ezekiel was among the Jews taken into Babylonian exile in 597 B.C. There in the environs of Babylon he was called to be a prophet in 593 B.C. and continued his ministry among the captives for at least two decades (Ezek. 1:1, 29:17).

The glory of the Babylonian kingdom began to fade with the death of Nebuchadnezzar in 562 B.C. His marked success had enlarged the small kingdom of Babylon to span the Near East from Susa to the Mediterranean, from the Persian Gulf to the upper Tigris, and from the Taurus Mountains down to the first cataract in Egypt. As an adventurous builder he made the city of Babylon the mightiest fortress in the world, adorned with unsurpassed splendor and beauty. The power and genius that characterized his 43-year reign were never equaled by any of his successors.

Awel-Marduk, also known as Evil-Merodach, ruled for only two years over the empire he inherited from his father. Although the Jewish historian Josephus appraises him as a harsh ruler, the Scriptures indicate his generosity toward Jehoiachin. This former king of Judah who had been taken into exile in 597 B.C. was now released at the age of fifty-five (cf. Jer. 52:31–34, 2 Kings 25:27–30). Awel-Marduk's reign was abruptly terminated when he was murdered by Neriglissar, who was enthroned on August 13, 560 B.C.

Neriglissar came to the throne either by dint of his leading a revolution supported by the priests and the army or as heir by virtue of his marriage to Nebuchadnezzar's daughter. It is highly probable that he is correctly identified with Nergal-sharezer, the "Rab-mag," or chief officer, who released Jeremiah in 586 B.C. after the conquest of Jerusalem (Jer. 39:3, 13). In his building activities he restored the Esagila temple of Marduk at Babylon, the Ezida temple of Nebo at Borsippa, and the chapel of destiny (focal point of the New Year's festival at Babylon), repaired an old palace, and built canals as any king was expected to do. Vigorous and aggressive, he maintained control throughout the empire. After his death in 556 B.C. his young son, Labashi-Marduk, was deposed and killed after reigning a few months, and Nabonidus seized the throne.

Nabonidus, claiming that he was the rightful successor to the Babylonian throne, duly recognized Marduk at the New Year's festival on March 31, 555 B.C., by participating as king and providing elaborate gifts for the Esagila temple. His religious interests, however, were rooted in Haran, where he restored the cult of the moon-god Sin in a new temple. Failing to appear in the Marduk procession in Babylon for several years, he offended not only the priests but also the commercial leaders in this great city. As a result, by 548 B.C. Nabonidus was forced to delegate his authority to Belshazzar and retire to Tema in Arabia. Here he manifested an interest in the caravan trade as well as in the promotion of the moon-god cult. Having disregarded the city of Babylon, Nabonidus attempted to maintain the empire from Tema.

By 550 B.C. Cyrus, who had come to the Persian throne as a vassal of Media (559 B.C.), had rebelled against Media, gained control of Ecbatana, and laid claim to Median rule over Assyria and beyond in the Fertile Crescent. Three years later he defeated Croesus of Lydia in a decisive battle, capturing him at Sardis in 547 B.C. As Cyrus extended his empire, cities such as Susa, under Gobryas' leadership, rebelled against the Babylonians. Nabonidus rescued some of the gods in these cities and brought them to Babylon. On New Year's Day in April 539, Nabonidus made an attempt to celebrate this festival properly after having neglected it for years, but the priests of Marduk and Nebo did not enthusiastically rally to the king's support. By October 11, 539, the city of Sippar had surrendered to Cyrus without a battle. Two days later Gobryas took Babylon with the troops of Cyrus. Belshazzar was slain; Nabonidus may have escaped but was subsequently captured and apparently received favorable treatment after his release. Before the end of October Cyrus himself entered Babylon as victor and conqueror.

It is during this period of Babylonian decline that Daniel's visions in chapters 7 and 8 can be dated, respectively, in 550 and 547 B.C.

With his lack of involvement in Babylonian affairs under Nabonidus and Belshazzar and his years of political experience, Daniel must have been apprehensive about Persia's rise to power while the Babylonian kingdom disintegrated under Nebuchadnezzar's successors. He was deeply troubled and appalled by his visions (7:25 and 8:27). On the eve of Babylon's conquest Daniel was called before Belshazzar to interpret God's solemn warning that he has been weighed in the balance and found wanting (5:1–30). Although Belshazzar was slain, Daniel was recognized as an outstanding administrator in kingdom affairs by Darius, the Mede who ruled in Babylon after its conquest by Cyrus (Dan. 6:1–28). During these crucial developments Daniel expressed his concern for the future of his people in a prayer of intercession and was divinely assured that God's plan of restoration would be fulfilled (Dan. 9:1–27). Daniel's last recorded divine revelation is dated in the third year of Cyrus (Dan. 10:1–12:13).

Cyrus the Great expanded Persia into a first-rate international power (559–530 B.C.). By securing Sardis and Miletus he resolved his encounter with the Greeks on the western frontier. In the east he marched his armies victoriously to the Oxus and Jaxartes rivers, extending Persian sovereignty to the borders of India and doubling the extent of his empire.

Restoration Under Persia

In Babylon Cyrus was hailed as a great liberator. The gods that had been taken there from the surrounding cities were restored to their local temples. Not only did Cyrus acknowledge Marduk as the god who had enthroned him as king in Babylon but he remained there for several months to celebrate the New Year's festival. This was a political expedient to assure him of popular support as he assumed control of the vast Babylonian empire, which extended west through Syria and Palestine to the borders of Egypt. Cyrus reversed the notorious Assyrian and Babylonian policy of taking conquered peoples to a foreign land, a ruthless practice initiated by Tiglath-pileser III in 745 B.C. He encouraged uprooted peoples to return to their homelands and restore the gods to their temples. To the Jews, who had been in exile since the beginning of Nebuchadnezzar's reign, Cyrus was a welcome deliverer.

The proclamation by Cyrus allowing the Jews to return to their homeland was read out in the Hebrew language to Jewish communities throughout the empire. Adapting it to their religion, Cyrus claimed that he was commissioned by the Lord God of heaven to build a temple at Jerusalem (Ezra 1:1–4). He encouraged those who remained to support the emigrants with offerings of gold, silver, beasts, and other supplies for the re-establishment of the Jerusalem Temple. Even as Cyrus had acknowledged Marduk when he entered Babylon, so here he gave recognition to the God of the Jews. Although this may have been merely political expediency on his part, he nevertheless fulfilled Isaiah's prediction that after their exile God would use Cyrus to bring the Jews back to their own land (Isa. 45:1–4).

Approximately fifty thousand exiles made the long, hazardous trek to Jerusalem, intent on rebuilding the Temple that had been in ruins for approximately fifty years (Ezra 1:5–2:70). Under orders by Cyrus the vessels that Nebuchadnezzar had taken from the Temple were entrusted to Sheshbazzar, a prince of Judah, for transportation to Jerusalem. Unique among the nations, the Jews had no statue of their God to be restored, although this provision was included in the general decree made by Cyrus. The ark of the covenant, which was the most sacred object Israel possessed, had undoubtedly been lost in the destruction of Jerusalem.

After settling in the environs of Jerusalem, the returned exiles gathered en masse to build the altar of the God of Israel and re-establish the burnt offerings as prescribed by Moses (Exod. 29:38 ff.). Then they observed the Feast of Booths, or Tabernacles (cf. Lev. 23:34 ff.). Plans then were made to rebuild the Temple, including negotiating with the Phoenicians for building materials in accordance with the permission granted by Cyrus (Ezra 3:1–4:23). Construction was begun under Zerubbabel, a grandson of Jehoiachin, representing the house of David in political leadership, and Joshua the high priest officiating in religious matters. Hostile opposition from the officials in Samaria, however, successfully hindered the work on the Temple throughout the rest of the reign of Cyrus and the reign of Cambyses, even until the second year of the reign of Darius (520 B.C.).

Cyrus was fatally wounded in battle while he was leading his army to the northern frontier west of the Caspian Sea beyond the Araxes River. Cambyses had his body taken back to Pasargadae, the Persian capital, for burial in the tomb that Cyrus had constructed for himself. When Alexander the Great, two centuries later, found this tomb vandalized, he ordered its restoration. Today the empty tomb bears witness to the greatness of Cyrus, who won for the Persians their empire but eventually was begrudged the resting place he had so elaborately prepared.

When Cyrus left Babylon in 538 B.C. he appointed his son Cambyses to represent the Persian king in the royal processions on New Year's Day. By duly recognizing Marduk, Nebo, and Bel and by retaining the officers and palace dignitaries of Babylon, Cambyses became well established in Babylonia, with headquarters at Sippar.

With the sudden death of Cyrus in 530 Cambyses asserted himself as king of Persia. After he secured recognition from the many provinces his father had brought under Persian control, Cambyses turned his attention to the conquest of Egypt, which still lay beyond the bounds of the empire. In the battle of Pelusium (525 B.C.) he decisively defeated the Egyptians and appropriated for himself the titles of Egyptian kingship. Cultivating friendship with the Greeks, he extended Persian dominion over the more advanced and wealthiest half of the Greek world through lucrative trade. Returning from Egypt in 525 B.C. Cambyses was so disturbed by news that Gaumata had seized the Persian throne that he committed suicide near Mount Carmel in Palestine.

Darius I, also known as Darius the Great (522–486 B.C.), saved the empire in this time of crisis. Having served Cambyses as spearbearer, Darius quickly rushed eastward from Mount Carmel, executed Gaumata and seized the Persian throne. Three months later rebellious Babylon came under his control. After two years of hard fighting he dissipated all opposition in Armenia and Media. He returned to Egypt as king in 519–518 B.C. What contact he had en route with the Jewish settlement at Jerusalem is not known.

The Temple Rebuilt—Ezra 1–6

In 521 B.C. the Jews in Jerusalem made an appeal to Darius and secured his permission and support to rebuild the Temple (Ezra 5:1–6:22). Haggai, with God's message for the occasion, stirred up the people and leaders by reminding them that they had become so absorbed in building their own houses that they had neglected the place of worship. In less than a month's time Zerubbabel and Jeshua led the people in a renewed effort to rebuild the Temple (Hag. 1:1–15). Shortly thereafter the prophet Zechariah collaborated with Haggai in stimulating the building program (Zech. 1:1).

The resumption of building activities in Jerusalem was challenged by Tattenai, the satrap of Syria, and his colleagues, who represented the interests of Persia in this area. Responding to their appeal, Darius ordered a search in the archives in Babylonia and Ecbatana, capital of Media. Darius then not only confirmed the edict by Cyrus but instructed the governors in the Trans-Euphrates area to support the Jews with royal revenue and building supplies. Consequently Tattenai's appeal, which was intended to be injurious, providentially resulted in providing not only the political support of Darius but also the material aid from the immediate district officials for the project.

The Temple was completed in five years, 520–515 B.C. Although erected on the same site, it could not have equaled in beauty or workmanship the structure built by Solomon after David's elaborate preparation and with his unequaled resources. This Temple was dedicated with impressive and elaborate ceremonies. The last offering signified that this worship represented the entire nation of Israel, with whom the covenant was made. With this dedication service the priests and Levites initiated their regular services in the sanctuary as prescribed for them the law of Moses. The next month the Jews observed the Passover. Israelites who were still living in Palestine joined the returned exiles in these joyous celebrations, renouncing their heathen practices and renewing their allegiance to God as they worshiped in the Temple.

The dedication of the Temple and the observance of the Passover in the spring of 515 B.C. marked a historic point in Jerusalem. The hopes of the exiles had been realized in re-establishing the Temple as their place of worship. At the same time as they were reminded by the Passover of Israel's redemption from Egyptian bondage, they enjoyed the reality of restoration from Babylon.

In 513 B.C. Darius marched his armies westward across the Bosporus and the Danube to meet the Scythians coming down from the steppes of Russia. This venture proved unsuccessful, but he returned to add Thrace to his empire and spent the next three years in Sardis. This initiated a series of conflicts with the Greeks that ultimately proved disastrous for the Persians. The westward advance of the Persians was abruptly halted in a crucial defeat at the Marathon in 490 B.C.

Darius was a genius in administration and in the organization of his empire. He had an exceptional flare for architecture, reflected in his numerous building projects in capital cities and elsewhere. Ecbatana, the former Median capital, became a favorite royal summer home. Susa, sixty miles north of the mouth of the Tigris, was centrally located for administrative purposes and served as a choice winter residence.

Persepolis was developed by Darius as the most impressive capital of the Persian empire. It was built on the crest of the "Mountain of Mercy," with a row of walls and towers beyond which was the vast plain now known as Marv Dasht. The palace of Darius, the Tachara, was begun by him in 520 B.C. and completed and enlarged by succeeding rulers. Columns of this tremendous structure still bear testimony to Persian construction and art. Persepolis was strategically fortified with a triple defense. In a cliff near Persepolis Darius prepared an elaborately carved rock tomb for himself. In the far distant land of Egypt he promoted the construction of a canal between the Red Sea and the Nile.

Xerxes I (486–465 B.C.) was heir-elect to the Persian throne when Darius died. For twelve years he had served as viceroy at Babylon under the rule of his father. When he took over the empire there were incomplete building projects, religious reforms, and rebellions in various parts of the domain awaiting his attention. In 482 B.C. he punished rebellious Babylon by destroying the fortifications erected by Nebuchadnezzar, razing the Esagila temple and melting the pound solid gold statue of Marduk for bullion. Babylon lost its identification by being incorporated into Assyria.

Directing his energy toward the expansion of the western frontier, Xerxes led his enormous Persian army toward Greece with the support of his navy, composed of Phoenician, Greek, and Egyptian units. The army suffered reverses at Thermopylae; the fleet was defeated at Salamis; and finally the Persians were decisively routed at Plataea and Cape Mycale. In 479 Xerxes retreated to Persia, abandoning the conquest of Greece.

Queen Esther—Esther 1–10

Xerxes is mentioned in the Book of Esther, the main biblical source for the period of Jewish history from the time of the completion of the Temple under Darius (515 B.C.) to the reign of Artaxerxes in 464 B.C. Dated events in this account refer to the third, seventh, and twelfth years of Xerxes' reign (cf. Esther 1:3; 2:16; 3:7).

Susa, which had shared the distinction of being a royal city with Babylon and Ecbatana since the days of Cyrus, is the geographical point of interest in Esther; the magnificent palace of Xerxes occupied 2.5 acres of the acropolis of this great Elamite city. Displeased with Vashti as his queen, Xerxes banished her from the royal court. In due time Esther was chosen and publicly acknowledged as queen at a royal banquet before the princes. She was taken to King Xerxes in the royal residence in the seventh year of his reign, or about the time he returned from his unsuccessful venture to conquer Greece.

Mordecai, Esther's cousin, kept in close contact with her throughout this period. Lingering near the royal court, he learned that two palace guards were conspiring to kill the king. Through Esther this was reported to the king, and the culprits were hanged. In the meantime Haman, an influential member of Xerxes' court, became incensed that Mordecai refused to do obeisance. Knowing that Mordecai was a Jew, Haman developed plans for the execution of the Jews and had them approved by the king.

Wherever this decree was made public the Jews responded with fasting and mourning, including Mordecai, who appeared at the palace gate in sackcloth and ashes. Esther, whose Jewish identity had been concealed, yielded to Mordecai's plea that she should approach the king on behalf of her people, even though to do so was to risk her life. Given the king's favor, Esther invited Xerxes and Haman to a banquet and requested them to return the next day. When the Xerxes could not sleep that night, he learned from the official records that Mordecai had uncovered the conspiracy against him. Consequently that day the king instructed Haman to honor Mordecai publicly. At dinner that night Esther, in the presence of Haman, courageously implored the king to save her and her people from annihilation. When she identified Haman as the culprit, Xerxes ordered his execution. Ironically Haman was hanged on the gallows he had prepared for Mordecai.

The edict for the annihilation of the Jews was annulled, and Mordecai became an influential member of Xerxes' court. With the king's approval Mordecai issued a new edict stating that the Jews should avenge themselves of any enemies that might attack them. The Jews were so jubilant at this announcement that many began to fear the consequences. Not a few people took up the outward forms of the Jewish religion in order to avoid violence. In the fighting that broke out thousands of non-Jews were slain. Peace was quickly restored, however, and the Jews instituted an annual celebration to commemorate their deliverance. Purim was the name for this holiday, because Haman had determined this date by casting the lot, or Pur.

Xerxes resumed his building program after returning from his unsuccessful venture to Greece. In Persepolis he completed the

Apadana; thirteen of the seventy-two pillars upholding the roof of this spacious audience hall still stand. In sculpture, Xerxes displayed Persian art at its best by adorning the stairway of the Apadana with magnificent sculptured figures of Susian and Persian guards. Although Xerxes was inferior as a military leader and will always be remembered for his defeat in Greece, he overshadowed his predecessors as a builder. It was to his credit that Persepolis became the outstanding city of the Persian kings, excelling in sculpture and architecture.

In 465 B.C. Xerxes was assassinated by Artabanus, the head of the palace guard. He was buried in the rock-hewn tomb that he had excavated next to that of Darius the Great.

Artaxerxes I (464-425 B.C.), with the support of the assassin Artabanus, seized the throne of his father. After disposing of other aspirants to the throne, he successfully suppressed rebellions in Egypt (460 B.C.) and a revolt in Syria (448). The Athenians negotiated a treaty with him by which both parties agreed to maintain the status quo. Not a dynamic ruler, Artaxerxes enjoyed life in his palace cities and entrusted military campaigns to his generals and the rule of the provinces to friends and relatives.

Ezra the Scribe—Ezra 7-10

It was during the reign of Artaxerxes that Ezra, a pious Levite of the Aaronic family, devoted himself to the study of the Torah while living with exiles in Babylonia. His interest in mastering the law of Moses found expression in a teaching ministry to his people. In his eagerness to return to Palestine, he appealed to Artaxerxes and subsequently was commissioned to lead a large company of Jews from exile to their homeland in Palestine (Ezra 7:1-10:44). He was empowered by the king to appoint magistrates and judges in the Jewish province, confiscate property, and imprison or execute anyone who did not conform.

Artaxerxes made most generous financial provision for Ezra's mission. Generous royal contributions, freewill offerings contributed by the exiles, and vessels for sacred use were given to Ezra for the Jerusalem Temple. Artaxerxes had such confidence in Ezra that he gave him a blank check on the royal treasury for anything he deemed necessary for temple service. Provincial rulers beyond the Euphrates were ordered to supply Ezra with food and money lest the royal family incur the wrath of Israel's God. Furthermore, all those engaged in temple service in Jerusalem—singers, servants, doorkeepers, and priests—were exempt from taxation. After appealing to God for divine protection, Ezra, with a company of eighteen hundred men and their families, made the long and treacherous trek of nearly a thousand miles to their homeland. Three and a half months later they arrived in Jerusalem.

Soon after his arrival Ezra was informed that Israelites had been guilty of intermarriage with heathen inhabitants. Even religious and civil leaders were among the participants. Ezra not only tore his garments to signify his deep grief but pulled his hair to express his moral indignation and wrath. Shocked and stunned, he sat in the Temple court while people who feared the consequences gathered around him. At the time of the evening sacrifice he rose from his fasting and with torn garments knelt in prayer, audibly confessing Israel's sin as a great crowd joined him in praying and weeping.

In response to a public proclamation throughout the land, the people assembled three days later in the open square before the Temple. Impressed with the seriousness of their offense, the people agreed to let the officials represent them so that the congregation could be dismissed, since it was the rainy season. Assisted by a select group of men and aided by representatives from various parts of the Jewish state, Ezra conducted a three-month examination. An impressive list of priests, Levites, and laity, totaling 114, was found guilty of intermarriage. Sacrificing a ram for a guilt offering, the guilty parties made a solemn pledge to annul their marriages.

Nehemiah—Nehemiah 1–13

About thirteen years after Ezra's arrival, Nehemiah came to Jerusalem to serve as governor of Judah, beginning in 444 B.C. (Neh. 1:1–13:31). In 432 B.C. (13:6) he returned to Persia. How soon he came back to Jerusalem or how long he continued as governor is not indicated. The events related in chapters 1–12 could all have occurred during the first year of his governorship. Nehemiah, one of the most colorful figures in the postexilic era, forfeited his position as cupbearer at the Persian court to serve his own nation in the rebuilding of Jerusalem. His physical handicap (he was a eunuch) became an asset in devoted service and distinguished leadership during the years that he was active as governor.

Living in Susa and serving in a high-ranking position in the royal court of Artaxerxes, Nehemiah had been grief-stricken to hear that the walls of Jerusalem were still in ruins. After three months of prayer and fasting he had had the opportunity to share this concern with the king. Artaxerxes not only duly authorized Nehemiah to go on this mission but issued letters in his behalf, sending orders to the governors beyond the Euphrates to supply him with building materials for the walls and gates of the city as well as his own private home.

Nehemiah's arrival at Jerusalem complete with army officers and cavalry alarmed the surrounding governors. Accompanied by a small committee, Nehemiah promptly made a nocturnal tour of the city, inspecting the condition of the walls. He then gathered the people and confronted them with the proposal to rebuild the walls. Enthusiastically they rallied to his support. An efficient organizer, Nehemiah then assigned people to various gates and sections of the walls.

Such sudden and intensive activity aroused opposition from surrounding provinces. Influential leaders, like Sanballat the Horonite, Tobiah the Ammonite, and Geshem the Arab, charged the Jews with rebellion as soon as the work began. When they realized that the reparation project was progressing rapidly, they were enraged to the point of organizing resistance. Sanballat and Tobiah, supported by the Arabs, the Ammonites, and the Ashdodites, made plans to attack Jerusalem.

By this time the walls were completed to half their height. Nehemiah not only prayed but assigned guards day and night. Along the lowest parts of the walls, guard duty was allotted to various families. Upon realizing that their enemies were frustrated in their scheme by this efficient and effective guard system, the Jews resumed their building efforts. One half of the people continued their repairs with sword in readiness while the other half remained on active guard duty. Furthermore, at the sound of the trumpet, everyone was under orders to rush immediately to the point of danger to resist enemy attack. None of the laborers was allowed to leave Jerusalem. They worked from dawn to dark and remained on guard during the night.

This intensive effort to complete the reparation was especially difficult for the poorer classes of people. Economically they found it hard to pay taxes and interest and support their families while helping to rebuild the walls. Some even faced the prospect of enslaving their children to discharge their mounting debts. Immediately Nehemiah called a public assembly and exacted a promise from the offenders to return to the needy people that which had been taken. Interest payments were canceled. As administrator Nehemiah himself set the example. He did not collect from the people his gubernatorial allowance in food and money during the twelve years of his first term as his predecessors had done. In addition, 150 Jews and officials who frequented Jerusalem were guests at Nehemiah's table without charge. Neither he nor his servants acquired mortgages on land by the loan of money and corn as they helped the needy. In this way Nehemiah effectively dealt with the economic crisis during the crucial days of reparation.

When the enemies of the Jews heard that the walls were nearing completion in spite of their opposition, they devised numerous plans to ensnare Nehemiah. Repeatedly he repelled these successfully and uttered prayers that God might strengthen him in his responsibility. Nor was he intimidated when they sent a false prophet.

In spite of all this opposition, the walls of Jerusalem were completed in fifty-two days. The enemies lost face, and surrounding nations were duly impressed, realizing anew that God had favored Nehemiah. The successful termination of Nehemiah's reparation project in the face of enemy opposition established the respect and prestige of the Jewish state among the provinces west of the Euphrates.

With Jerusalem securely enclosed, Nehemiah set up a guard system to prevent enemy attack. Civilians living within the city were charged with guard duty during the night at parts of the walls near their own homes. Faced with sparsely settled areas in Jerusalem, Nehemiah called for a registration of the people throughout the province in order to recruit some for settlement within the city. During the seventh month his program gave precedence to religious activities as the people observed the Feast of Trumpets, the Day of Atonement, and the Feast of Tabernacles. Since he was not a priest Nehemiah receded into the background during the religious activities, being mentioned only twice in Nehemiah 8–10.

Ezra, the priest and scribe, emerges as the outstanding religious leader. As a renowned teacher of the law, since his return he undoubtedly had assembled the people annually for these festive celebrations. This year the people had reason to make it the greatest celebration ever. Behind the closed walls of Jerusalem they could gather in peace and safety without the fear of enemy attack. The morale of the people must have been strengthened by Nehemiah's successful leadership.

Standing on a wooden platform, from dawn to midday Ezra read the law of Moses to the standing congregation assembled in the Water Gate Square for the observance of the Feast of Trumpets. When the reading moved the people to tears, Nehemiah, supported by Ezra and the teaching Levites, admonished them to rejoice and make this a festive occasion by sharing the prepared food in common fellowship. Then they enthusiastically made preparation to celebrate the Feast of Tabernacles as prescribed in Leviticus (23:39–43). So widespread was the participation that this proved to be the outstanding observance of the Feast of Tabernacles since the days of Joshua, who had led Israel in the conquest of Canaan.

On the eighth day, after the law had been read publicly for seven days, there was a holy convocation with the offering of prescribed sacrifices. After a one-day intermission the people assembled for prayer and fasting as Ezra and assisting Levites led the people in the reading of the law, confession of sin, and the offering of thanks to God. In a written covenant, signed by Nehemiah and other representatives of the congregation, the people bound themselves by an oath to keep the law of God that had been given by Moses. Two laws were singled out for emphasis: intermarriage with heathen and the keeping of the Sabbath. The implications of this commitment were realistic and practical. As the people acknowledged their obligations to give the tithe, the firstfruits, the firstborn, and other contributions prescribed by the law, the needs of the Temple ministry were met.

After this Nehemiah resumed the execution of his plan for increasing the population of Jerusalem, ensuring civil defense. The dedication of the walls of Jerusalem involved the entire province. Two processions, one led by Nehemiah and the other by Ezra, marched on the walls of Jerusalem, meeting at the Temple for a great service of thanksgiving with music furnished by an orchestra and choirs. Abundant sacrifices were presented as an expression of joy and thanksgiving. So extensive and joyous was the celebration that the triumphant noise was heard afar.

As an efficient administrator Nehemiah organized the priests and Levites to take care of the tithes and other contributions made by the people. From various provincial towns these gifts were properly channeled to Jerusalem through responsible Levites so that the priests and Levites could effectively perform their duties. The singers and gatekeepers also received their regular support so that they could serve as prescribed by David and Solomon (2 Chron. 8:14). As the people rejoiced in the ministry of the priests and Levites, they willingly supported the Temple ministry.

During his twelfth year as governor of Judah (ca. 432 B.C.) Nehemiah made a trip back to Persia. The length of his stay is not indicated, but when he returned he was indignant to find religious laxity. Provisions for the Temple ministry had not been provided, and the Temple had been neglected and desecrated. Men who were considered trustworthy were appointed over the storehouses so that the Levites again received their allotments.

Sabbath observance was next on Nehemiah's reform list. He ordered that the Jerusalem gates be closed on the Sabbath to terminate the promtion of business on this day. He assigned his own servants as guards to stop commercial traffic, warning the merchants not to arrive at the gates of Jerusalem on the Sabbath. He also dealt with the problem of mixed marriages. Taking drastic action, he expelled from Judah the grandson of Eliashib the high priest. He had married the daughter of Sanballat, governor of Samaria, who had caused Nehemiah no end of trouble during the first year when the Jews were repairing the walls of Jerusalem.

With a brief summary of the religious reforms and provisions for proper Temple service, Nehemiah concludes the account of his activities in the Book of Nehemiah. Earnestly zealous for the cause of God, he utters a final prayer: "Remember me, O my God, for good."

For additional study help see *Figures 10* and *11* in the Appendix.

Chapter 11

INTERPRETATION OF LIFE

Five literary units commonly known as poetical books are Job, Psalms, Proverbs, Ecclesiastes, and the Song of Solomon. None of these could be properly classified as historical or prophetical books. As part of the Old Testament canon they provide additional insight into the life of the Israelites.

These books cannot be dated with certainty, since allusions to historical data are limited in this literature. Kings, prophets, philosophers, poets, common people—all are represented among the contributors, many of whom are anonymous.

Reflected in this literature are the problems, experiences, beliefs, philosophies, and attitudes of the Israelites. Such a wide variety of interests are expressed that these writings have a well-nigh universal appeal. Their frequent use by the common people throughout the world and the voluminous literature written since Old Testament times indicate that the poetical books deal with problems and truths familiar to all humanity. Notwithstanding differences in time, culture, and civilization, the basic ideas expressed by the Israelite writers in their interpretation of life are still vitally important to people everywhere.

Job—The Problem of Suffering

Human suffering, the age-old question, has continued to be an unsolved problem. Nor does the Book of Job provide a final solution. However, significant truths are projected in this extended discussion.

Regarded as a unit this book in its present form may be appropriately designated is an epic-drama. Although the main part of the composition is poetical and in the form of a debate, the framework is a prose narrative that provides the basis for the whole discussion. Neither its historical background nor the time of composition of this book can be ascertained with certainty. The author remains anonymous.

The Book of Job has been recognized as one of the greatest productions of all time. Among the Hebrew writers the author of this book displays the most extensive vocabulary—he is at times referred to as the Shakespeare of the Old Testament. Exhibited in this book are vast resources of knowledge, a superb style of forceful expression, profundity of thought, excellent command of language, noble ideals, a high standard of ethics, and a genuine love for nature. The religious and philosophical ideas have claimed the consideration of great theologians and philosophers down to the present day.

The beginning reader should consider the book as a unit, but to guide the reader in understanding the message, the book may be subdivided as follows:

Introduction or historical setting	1:1–3:26
The dialogue with his three friends	4:1–31:40
The speeches of Elihu	32:1–37:24
The speeches of the Almighty	38:1–41:34
The conclusion	42:1–17

Job's homeland was in the land of Uz. Although specific chronological data are lacking, the times in which Job lived seem to fit best into the patriarchal era. The misfortunes of this just man provide the setting for the dialogue that constitutes the major part of the book.

Vividly the man Job is portrayed in three different situations: in times of unprecedented prosperity, extreme poverty, and immeasurable personal suffering. The faith of Job reaches beyond the mundane to an eternal hope. Even though the latter is not clearly delineated, Job does not utterly despair during his crucial time of suffering.

Job is described as a God-fearing man whose equal was nowhere to be found in the human race. The high standard of ethics by which he lived was beyond the realization of most people (29–31). Even after his friends had scrutinized his whole pattern of behavior, Job's moral conduct remained beyond reproach.

Though he was the wealthiest man in the East, Job did not allow material possessions to obscure his devotion to God. In times of feasting he continually made sacrifices for the welfare of his family. His use of his wealth for aiding the needy is reflected throughout the rest of the book.

Suddenly Job is reduced to extreme poverty. In four catastrophic developments he loses all his material possessions. Two of these misfortunes apparently came from natural sources—attacks by the Sabeans and the Chaldeans. The other two—a consuming fire and a great wind—were beyond human control. Job not only was bankrupted materially but lost all his children.

Job was dumbfounded—he tore his clothes and shaved his head. Then he turned to God in worship. Recognizing that all he owned had come to him from God, he also acknowledged that in the providence of God he had lost everything. For this he blessed God, charging him with no wrong.

Afflicted with terrible boils, Job seated himself on an ash heap and desperately sought relief by scraping himself with potsherd. At this point his wife advised him to curse God and die. Once again this righteous man rose above circumstances and acknowledged God as the controller of the fortunes of life.

Three friends—Eliphaz, Bildad, and Zophar—came to call on Job with the avowed purpose of comforting him. They hardly recognized him in his state of suffering. So stunned were these three that they sat in silence for seven days. Job finally broke the stillness by cursing the day of his birth—nonexistence would be better than to endure such suffering. In anguish of soul and physical torment he pondered the enigma of his existence in the question, Why was I ever born?

The underlying problem in the entire discussion is that neither Job nor his friends know the reason for these apparent misfortunes. Unknown to them were the developments behind the scenes. Satan appeared before God to challenge Job's devotion and faith. He made the accusation that Job simply served God for material reward; he was granted permission to strip the richest man in the East of all earthly possessions but not permitted to harm Job himself. When Job's resultant philosophy of life did not bear out Satan's wager, God granted the accuser liberty to afflict Job himself but with specific restrictions to spare his life. Even though Job cursed the day of his birth, he never cursed God. Fully conscious of his suffering and having no explanation, Job raised the question "Why?" as he delved into the mystery of his peculiar lot in life.

In the first cycle of speeches (4–14) his friends fail to recognize Job's genuine devotion to God and assume that he is suffering for his sin. Job agrees with them that God is omnipotent, omniscient, and righteous. With an intense longing for God, but not realizing temporary relief, Job sinks into the depths of despair, wondering if there is a life after death.

In the second cycle (15–21) his friends charge Job with arrogance and insist that common knowledge teaches that suffering is the result of sin. They infer that Job must be a sinner since it is very evident that he is suffering. Forsaken by his friends, alienated from his family, abhorred by his wife, and ignored by his servants, Job portrays his lonely suffering under the hand of God. Only by faith does he reach beyond his present circumstances. He anticipates future vindication on the basis of his record as he confidently expresses his hope in the words, "I know that my Redeemer lives." Job takes issue with the conclusion of his friends that wicked people always suffer. Many wicked people prosper, enjoy life to the full, are given an honorable burial, and are respected for their success. This is confirmed by observers who have a broad knowledge of people and affairs.

In the third cycle (22–31) Job's friends, expressing their firm belief that suffering is the result of sin, feel compelled to conclude that Job is a sinner. Boldly they charge him with secret sins. Job is baffled. His suffering continues while heaven remains silent. A sense of urgency and impatience overwhelms him as he does not see God act in his behalf. All he has done is fully known to the One whom he has faithfully served in faith and obedience. At the same time injustice, violence, and iniquity continue as God sustains the life of the wicked.

Job concurs with his friends that human beings are inferior to God. Asserting that he is innocent and that they are wrong in their charges, he portrays the lot of the wicked. They have no guarantee of lasting prosperity. Although human beings have explored and harnessed the resources of nature, they are still baffled in their search for wisdom. It cannot be purchased, although God has demonstrated his wisdom in the universe. Can humanity find it? Only the God-fearing, moral person has access to that wisdom and understanding (28).

Job concludes by reviewing his whole case. He contrasts the golden days of extreme happiness, prosperity, and prestige with his present state of suffering, contempt, and anguish of soul in the consciousness that his lot has been ordained by God. In considerable detail Job recounts his standard of ethics and integrity in dealing with his fellow human beings. Untainted by immorality, vanity, thoughtlessness, covetousness, idolatry, bitterness, and insincerity, Job pleads innocence. Neither God nor any person sustain the charges his friends have leveled against him (29–31).

Elihu, being younger, had refrained from speaking, until he is compelled to utter what he discerns as the truth of God. With a tender sensitivity toward sin and a genuine reverence for God, Elihu suggests the sublimity of God as a teacher who seeks to discipline. The greatness of God displayed in nature is overwhelming. Human understanding of God's ways is conditioned by the limitations of the human mind. How can human beings understand God aright? Therefore we should not be wise in our own conceit but fear him who is great in power, justice, and righteousness (32–37).

In a multitude of words neither Job nor his friends have solved the problem of retribution, the mystery of suffering, or the disciplinary designs in Job's particular lot in life. Neither have the speeches of the Almighty presented a reasoned argument that would afford a detailed, logical explanation (38–41). The wonders of the physical universe and the marvels of the animal kingdom displayed God's wisdom beyond any conception or understanding. Even Job, who has answered his friends repeatedly, humbly acknowledges that he cannot reply to God.

Job is overrwhelmed with the wisdom and power of God. Who should doubt the propriety of God's ways in the suffering of the righteous or the prosperity of the wicked? The secrets and motives of God in his justice toward humanity are beyond human appraisal. In dust and ashes Job humbly bows in worship, confessing his insignificance. In a new perspective on God as well as himself, he realizes that he has spoken beyond his limited knowledge and understanding. By faith and confidence in God, he surmounts the limitations of human reason in his solution to the problems he so boldly raised before the silence of heaven was broken (42:1–6).

Identified by God as "my servant," Job became the officiating priest and intercessor for his three friends who had spoken so foolishly. His fortunes were restored in double measure. In the fellowship of his relatives and friends, Job was comforted and blessed by God after this time of severe testing.

Psalms—Hymnology of Israel

For more than two millennia the Book of Psalms has been the most popular collection of writings in the Old Testament canon. The psalms were used in worship services by the Israelites beginning in Davidic times. The Christian church has incorporated the psalms in liturgy and ritual throughout the centuries. Throughout history, the Book of Psalms has merited more personal interest and greater usage in public worship than any other book in the Old Testament.

The popularity of the psalms rests in the fact that they reflect common human experience. Composed by numerous authors, the various psalms express the emotions, personal feelings, attitudes, gratitude, and interests of the average person. Universally people have identified their lot in life with that of the psalmists. David, who introduced the singing of songs in the house of the Lord (1 Chron. 6:31), is credited with seventy-three psalms. Among other authors are Asaph, the sons of Korah, Moses, Solomon, Heman, and Ethan.

About twenty-five psalms are anonymous. Ezra may have been the final editor of the Book of Psalms.

Subject matter seems to provide the best basis for a systematic study of the psalms, since each psalm, with few exceptions, is a single unit. They can be divided into various classifications according to their background of similar experience or their common theme.

Prayers of the righteous (Pss. 17, 20, 25, 28, 40, 42, 55, etc.) express the universal human need for deliverance. Pressed by anxiety, care, immediate danger, a concern for vindication, or the need for a revival, the longing soul humbly appeals to God for divine aid.

Penitential psalms (Pss. 6, 32, 38, 51, 102, etc.) most intensely express the inner longings of repentant individuals. Most of these are ascribed to David, who freely uttered his feelings in sincere confession of sin. Most exemplary is Psalm 51, for which historical background is provided in the title as well as in 2 Samuel 12:1-13. Fully conscious of his terrible guilt, which was expressed with a threefold emphasis—sin, iniquity, and transgression—David in no wise sought to evade accountability. Overwhelmed and utterly humbled, he turned to God in faith, realizing that a broken and contrite spirit are acceptable to God. The sacrifices of a penitent individual delight the God of Mercy. Psalm 32, related to the same experience, indicates the divine guidance and praise that becomes a reality in the life of one who has penitently confessed his or her sin.

Psalms of praise (Pss. 65, 95-100, 111-118, 146-150) are expressions of exultation and gratitude that often came as a natural consequence of a great deliverance. Thanksgiving for harvest, joy in adoration, festive celebrations, and the "Great Hallels" became important parts of the psalmody of Israel.

Pilgrim psalms (Pss. 120-134) are labeled "Songs of Ascents" or Songs of Degrees" in our English Bibles. Very likely they were associated with the annual pilgrimages of the Israelites to Zion for the three great festivals.

In historical psalms (Pss. 78, 105, 106, etc.), the psalmists reflect on God's dealings with Israel in days past. Israel had a history of varied experiences that furnished a rich background, inspiring poets and song writers. Throughout these psalms there are numerous references to the miraculous deliverances and divine favors afforded Israel in the past.

Messianic psalms prophetically indicated some aspect of the Messiah as he was revealed later in the New Testament. Outstanding in this classification is Psalm 22, which has several references that parallel the passion of Jesus as portrayed in the four Gospels. Although Psalms in this group reflect the emotional experiences of their author, their expressions, under divine inspiration, had prophetic import. Interrelated to the life and message of Jesus, this element in the psalms is vitally significant as interpreted in the New Testament. Vaguely expressed in psalms of worship, the messianic references became more apparent as they were fulfilled in Jesus, the Messiah.

With this analysis, the beginning reader will recognize that the Book of Psalms is as diverse as a church hymnal. Extended classification of the psalms necessarily increases duplication in the various categories. May the consideration thus far be but a beginning for further study of each individual psalm.

Proverbs—An Anthology of Israel

The Book of Proverbs is a superb anthology of wise sayings. Provocative in stimulating thought, a proverb points up a simple, self-evident truth. In popular use it often had an unfavorable connotation. The literary proverb, however, represents common-sense wisdom expressed in short, crisp form. In the course of time a proverb—*mashal* in Hebrew—not only became an effective tool of instruction but gained extensive use as a type of didactic discourse.

The association of wisdom with Solomon, to whom the major part of this collection is ascribed, is well attested in Kings and Chronicles. The historical accounts of this great king portray him as the embodiment of wisdom in the glory of Israel's most prosperous period. In humble dependence upon God, he began his reign with a prayer for wisdom. In his love for God, his concern to render righteous judgment, and the wise administration of his domestic and foreign affairs,

Solomon represented the essence of practical wisdom (1 Kings 3: 3-28; 4:29-30; 5:12). Surpassing all contemporary wise men, he gained such international fame that foreign rulers, notably the queen of Sheba, came to express their admiration and seek his wisdom (2 Chron. 9:1-24).

Versatile in literary efforts, Solomon gave discourses on subjects of common interest, such as plant and animal life He is credited with the composition of three thousand proverbs and a thousand and five songs; parts of the Book of Proverbs ascribed to him are but a sample of his words of wisdom.

The relationship between the Book of Proverbs and the wisdom of Amen-em-opet remains a problem for further study. Since Solomon's wisdom prevailed throughout the Fertile Crescent, it seems reasonable to consider seriously the possibility that Egyptian wisdom was influenced by the Israelites. The indebtedness of Amen-em-opet to Proverbs seems more likely if the former is dated at about 600 B.C., when the wise men had been active in Israel for several centuries.

The introduction (1:1-7) offers a statement of purpose for the entire collection. Although designed for youth, these proverbs offer wisdom for all. The key note is the "fear of the Lord"—wisdom begins with a right relationship with God. Personal acknowledgment of God is the foundation for righteous living. A reverence for God exemplified in daily life is the true application of wisdom.

A discussion of wisdom and folly is embodied in Proverbs 1:8-9:18. This is set forth in a teacher–pupil or father–son relationship, with the listener frequently addressed as "my son." From the school of experience come words of instruction to the youth venturing out on the untried ways of life. Wisdom, personified, speaks with irrefutable logic. It pleads with youth to consider all the advantages that wisdom offers and warns young people against the ways of folly, realistically pointing out the dangers of sexual crimes, bad company, and other deadly temptations. In a final appeal, wisdom spreads an enticing banquet table. Folly leads to ruin and death, but the votaries of wisdom are assured of God's favor.

The proverbs of Solomon preserved in Proverbs 10:1-22:16 consist of 375 verses, each of which normally constitutes a couplet. The vast majority are antithetical; others are comparisons or complementary statements. Various aspects of the behavior pattern of the wise and the foolish are brought into focus. Wealth, integrity, law observance, speech, honesty, arrogance, punishment, reward, politics, bribery, statesmanship, society, family life, reputation, character—almost every phase of life is portrayed in proper perspective.

The words of wisdom in Proverbs 22:17–24:34 contain instructive aphorisms. Dangers of oppression, etiquette at a royal table, the folly of teaching a fool, the fear of God, women, drunkenness, and the benefits of wisdom receive consideration in this teacher–pupil discourse.

Proverbs collected by the men of Hezekiah are grouped together in Proverbs 25–29. Probably the defeat of Sennacherib and the religious revival in the days of Hezekiah stimulated interest in this literary endeavor. It is not beyond possibility that Isaiah and Micah were in this group. These proverbs provide advice for kings and subjects, with special attention given to the behavior of fools. In the opportunities that life offers, the fool exhibits his folly, while the wise demonstrate their ways of wisdom.

The last two chapters are independent units. Agur, an unknown author, speaks of human limitations and the need for God's word as guidance. The final chapter opens with Lemuel's instructions for the king. In an alphabetic acrostic he lauds intelligent, industrious womanhood—a mother devoted to her home and children is praiseworthy.

Ecclesiastes—Investigation of life

Fascinating experiences and the philosophy of the author are propounded in the Book of Ecclesiastes. Speaking as "Koheleth," or "Teacher," he sets forth in prose and poetry his investigations and conclusions.

With the Teacher identifying himself as the son of David and ruling as king over Israel in Jerusalem, it seems reasonable to regard Solomon as the author of this book. A profound treatise, this book was classified with Job and Proverbs as wisdom literature of the Jews. It was publicly read at the Feast of Tabernacles and included in the Megilloth, or books used on feast days. The author's emphasis on the enjoyment of life made it appropriate reading at this annual season of rejoicing.

Ecclesiastes represents an expression of human ventures and failures. The author may not present a systematic philosophy such as Aristotle, Spinoza, Hegel, or Kant developed, but he makes a careful examination on the basis of observation and experience and then draws his own conclusions. As a whole he limits his investigation to things done "under the sun"—a frequently recurring phrase. Another expression, "all is vanity" (all is vapor, breath, or utterly meaningless), which occurs twenty-five times, gives the author's evaluation of the mundane things he considers. In his final deliberation he turned God-ward.

Skeptically this author poses the question, What is most worthwhile as life's objective? As in nature so in human life is there a repetitious cycle. (1:1–11). In this world there is nothing new. With this introduction he asserts that everything under the sun, or all activities limited to this life, are utterly meaningless.

In exploring the values of life Koheleth seeks after wisdom—but this seems to increase sorrow. As a cultured man he seeks to blend pleasure, laughter, and the enjoyment of gardens, mansions, wine, and music into one harmonious pattern of living, but this also is futile. In a sense it is paradoxical to pursue wisdom, since the wise endeavor to act in view of a future that is unknown. Why not live as the fool who lives only for today? But God has created and designed all things for human enjoyment. In the seemingly endless cycle of life there is a purpose for everything he has made, and ultimately human beings are accountable to God (1:12–3:22).

What bearing does economic status have on life? Who enjoys life more—the one who fulfills his or her given responsibilities as an ordinary servant or the industrious, aggressive individual who seeks to gain wealth and popularity? To practice religion as a matter of routine or hypocritically is not advantageous. Life's gains may bring ruin even to a king, since all are dependent on that which God provides in nature. The capacity to enjoy God's abundant provisions comes from God. Applied wisdom and temperance in all things are expedient. Unfortunately no finite creature achieves a perfectly balanced pattern of living, even though God created human beings upright in the beginning (4:1–7:29).

No one attains perfect wisdom in this life. Not knowing the future, one's analysis of life is definitely limited. When death summons us —be we righteous or wicked—we are helpless. In spite of the fact that death comes to all alike and that the universe appears indifferent to moral standards, it is still a matter of wisdom to fear God. We may not understand life—death is inevitable—but that should not keep us from enjoying life to the full. Wisdom, however, should be applied in all things. Noteworthy is the example of the poor man whose wisdom saved a city. Temperance in all things should regulate one's enjoyment of life. A little folly may bring much sorrow and deprive one of numerous benefits (8:1–10:20).

Certain principles and practices must be kept in mind. Share enjoyment with others, even though we know not the future. The Epicurean philosophy of living only for the present good is called into question. Let youth enjoy life to the fullest extent but remember that the final reckoning is with God. With a sobering allegory of old age, youth is warned to remember the Creator in the early years of life. The deterioration of the body organs or mental faculties may overtake one and render one incapable of taking God into consideration (11:1–12:12).

Significant is his final admonition: The duty of human beings is to fear or revere God and keep his commandments—the basis for our accountability to God (12:13–14).

The Song of Songs

The title of this book associates its composition with Israel's literary King Solomon. Among the numerous interpretations given to this book are: the allegorical view of Jews and Christians, the dramatic theory, the wedding-cycle theory, and the Adonis-Tammuz literature theory. At present there is no interpretation that has wide acceptance among Old Testament scholars.

Consensus of scholarship accords this song a high poetic quality as expressing the warm emotions of human love. Incorporated as a unit in the Jewish canon, it merits consideration as one single poem rather than a collection of songs. Component parts are monologues, soliloquies, and apostrophes. A variety of scenes—the royal court of Jerusalem, a garden, the countryside, or a pastoral surrounding—fit the settings of different parts of this poem, with the characters presented in quasi-dramatic action. Since so many details are missing in this song of love, the interpreter faces numerous problems.

The literal seems most natural to the reader. The principal figure seems to be a Shulammith maiden who is transferred from a pastoral environment to the royal palace of Solomon. As the king woos this attractive country lass, his overtures are rejected. The splendor of the palace and the choral appeal of the court women fail to impress her. She passionately yearns for her lover. Ultimately her conflict is resolved as she declines the overtures of the king and returns to her shepherd hero.

The following outline may provide a guide for reading:

The Shulammith maiden in the royal court	1:1–2:7
The maiden in a country palace	2:8–3:5
The king's appeal	3:6–4:7
The maiden reflects	4:8–6:3
The king's renewed appeal	6:4–7:9
The reunion of the maiden and her lover	7:10–8:14

Although the literal interpretation speaks of human love, the providential inclusion of this book in the Jewish canon undoubtedly has a spiritual significance. Most likely the Jews recognized this, as they read the Song of Songs annually at the Passover observance, which reminded the Israelites of God's love for them in their deliverance from Egyptian bondage. For the Jews the marital love represented God's love for Israel, as indicated by Isaiah (50:1; 54:4–5), Jeremiah

(3:1-20), Ezekiel (16 and 23), and Hosea (1-3). The bond between Israel (the Shulammith maiden) and her shepherd lover (God) was so strong that no worldly appeal (the king) could alienate her from God. In the New Testament this relationship is paralleled by Christ and the Church. Based on the literal interpretation, the Song of Songs thus has a spiritual application in the New Testament as well as the Old.

Chapter 12

ISAIAH AND HIS MESSAGE

Little is known about Isaiah's lineage, birth, youth, or education beyond the fact that he was the son of Amoz. Apparently he was born and reared in Jerusalem. Since his call to the prophetic ministry is definitely dated in the year that Uzziah died (740 B.C.), it is reasonable to date his birth about 765–760 B.C.

Isaiah was born in days of prosperity. Judah was regaining its military and economic strength under the competent leadership of Uzziah. Previously the foolish policies of Amaziah had subjected Judah to invasion and oppression by Israel and possibly to the reproach of Amaziah's imprisonment. The latter event may have brought about the recognition of Uzziah as coruler as early as 792–791 B.C. With the change in kings in Israel, Amaziah was restored to the throne (782–781), only to be assassinated (768 B.C.). This gave Uzziah sole control of Judah and the opportunity to assert his effective leadership.

Ominous developments soon cast lengthening shadows across Judah's future hopes. In Samaria, Jeroboam's death in 753 was followed by revolution and bloodshed until Menahem seized the throne. In Judah, Uzziah was smitten with leprosy as a divine judgment for assuming priestly duties. Although Jotham was made coruler at this time (ca. 750 B.C.), Uzziah continued in active leadership. Economic prosperity prevailed as Judah extended its boundary southward to include Elath on the Gulf of Aqaba. To the east the Ammonites were tributary to Judah.

Most portentous was the rise of Tiglath-pileser III, or Pul, to the

Assyrian throne in 745 B.C. His subsequent conquest of Babylon precipitated a unified preparation by Palestinian rulers for Assyrian aggression. In 743–738 this expectation became a reality as the Assyrian army advanced westward in several campaigns. Pul reports in his annals that he defeated a Palestinian force under the leadership of Azariah or Uzziah of Judah. Menahem, the king of Israel, also made a heavy payment of tribute to the king of Assyria (2 Kings 15:19).

Under the threat of Assyrian aggression rapid changes occurred in Israel, and these undoubtedly had their repercussions in Judah. When Menaham died he was succeeded by his son Pekahiah, who was murdered by Pekah after a two-year rule. The latter seized the throne in Samaria in 740–739 and began an aggressive anti-Assyrian policy. The death of Uzziah, the most outstanding king of Judah since the days of David and Solomon, occurred the same year.

During this year of tension at home and abroad, the young man Isaiah received his prophetic call. It is likely that he had observed international developments with keen interest as Judah's hope for national survival faded before the advancing armies of Assyria. What Isaiah's religious attitude was at this time is not indicated. He may have been familiar with Amos and Hosea, who were active in the Northern Kingdom. As a youth he might have come in contact with Zechariah, the prophet who had such a favorable influence upon Uzziah. In this crucial year he was called to be a spokesman for God —to deliver God's message to a generation facing unprecedented historical developments.

While Pekah firmly resisted the Assyrians, a pro-Assyrian party was gaining power in Judah. Apparently this movement was responsible for elevating Ahaz to the throne in 736–735 B.C. when the Assyrian armies were active in Nal and Urartu. Ahaz may have precipitated the Assyrian invasion of Philistia in 734. At least, after their retreat Pekah of Samaria and Rezin of Damascus issued an ultimatum to Ahaz to join them in opposing Assyria. At this point Isaiah became involved. He was specifically commissioned to advise the king to rely on God (Isa. 7:1 ff.). Ignoring the prophet's advice, Ahaz made a treaty with Tiglath-pileser III. Although Judah was invaded by the Syro-Ephraimitic armies and lost Edom as a tributary, Ahaz survived with the advance of the Assyrian army. Successive Assyrian campaigns brought the conquest and capitulation of Syria in 732 B.C. Simultaneously Pekah was executed and replaced by Hoshea, who assured the Assyrian king of Israel's tribute. Ahaz met Tiglath-pileser at Damascus and sealed his alliance by introducing Assyrian cult worship in the Temple at Jerusalem.

Isaiah's activity during the rest of the reign of Ahaz is obscure. He must have shared the keen interest and anxiety of the citizens of Judah concerning the struggles at Samaria—about forty miles north of Jerusalem. When Shalmaneser succeeded Tiglath-pileser on the Assyrian throne, Hoshea terminated his subservience. Following a three-year siege by the Assyrians, Hoshea was killed and Samaria conquered by the invader in 722 B.C. Apparently Ahaz was able to maintain favorable diplomatic relations with Assyrian, thus preventing the invasion of Judah at this time. There is no indication that Ahaz ever acknowledged Isaiah as a true prophet.

A new day dawned for Isaiah with Hezekiah's accession (716–715 B.C.). Ahaz had defied the prophet by supporting idolastrous worship in the Temple, but Hezekiah pursued a radically different course of action. Enthusiastically he introduced reforms, repaired and cleansed the Temple, and issued invitations to Israelites from Beersheba to Dan to join in the religious activities at Jerusalem. Though Isaiah does not mention these reforms in his book, the national celebration of the Passover and the conformity to the law of Moses must have encouraged him concerning Judah's future.

Present-day knowledge of Judo-Assyrian relations during the reign of Sargon II (722–705 B.C.) is quite limited. In the biblical record Sargon is mentioned only once (Isa. 20:1). It is known that Ashdod was conquered by the Assyrians in 711 B.C. Isaiah warned his people that they should not look to Egypt for support even though Shabako, the Ethiopian, had successfully established the Twenty-fifth Dynasty the previous year. For three years Isaiah walked about barefoot and clad as a slave, explaining his action as symbolic of the fate of Egypt and Ethiopia. How foolish his people were to seek Egyptian aid in rebelling against Assyria! Apparently Hezekiah maintained favorable relations with Assyria during this period by paying tribute. Jerusalem, at least, was safe from attack at this time.

In the meantime Hezekiah was building his defenses. The Siloam tunnel was constructed so that Jerusalem would be assured of an adequate water supply in case of an extended siege. Long before this, in the days of Ahaz, Isaiah had boldly declared that Assyria would extend its conquest and control into the kingdom of Judah.

In the crucial developments that followed Sennacherib's rise to power in Assyria (705 B.C.) Isaiah had vital and timely advice for Hezekiah. Nationalism emerged in rebellions throughout the Assyrian empire. Not the least in Sennacherib's success in suppressing these uprisings was the replacement of Merodach-baladan by Bel-ibni on the Babylonian throne in 702. The next year the Assyrians directed their advance westward. Through miraculous intervention Hezekiah survived.

How long Isaiah lived is not known from existing records. Beyond his association with Hezekiah about 700 B.C. little evidence is available concerning his later years. With no scriptural evidence to the contrary it is reasonable to concur with the suggestions indicating that Isaiah continued his ministry into the reign of Manasseh. If the record of Sennacherib's death is acknowledged as Isaian in origin, then the prophet still lived in 680 B.C. to indicate what finally happened to the Assyrian king who spoke so disparagingly of the God in whom Hezekiah had placed his trust. Tradition credits Manasseh with the martyrdom of Isaiah—the prophet was sawn in two when he was discovered hiding in a hollow tree trunk. From the standpoint of longevity it is valid to project Isaiah's ministry into the days of Manasseh. That Isaiah was in his twenties when he received his prophetic call in 740 B.C. is a logical assumption. His age at the time of his death after 680 B.C. would not necessarily have taken him beyond his eighties.

The historicity of Isaiah has never been questioned. Jewish statements as early as the second century B.C. attribute the entire book bearing his name to him. The Dead Sea Scrolls, dating back to the same period, verify the fact that the entire book was considered a unit at that time. For a brief analysis to guide the reader, the Book of Isaiah will be considered as a literary unit.

The Book of Isaiah is one of the most comprehensive of all Old Testament books. In the Hebrew text Isaiah ranks fifth in length after Jeremiah, Psalms, Genesis, and Ezekiel. In the New Testament Isaiah is quoted by name twenty times, which exceeds the total number of references to all other writing prophets in New Testament books.

Various themes can be traced throughout this book. The attributes and characteristics of God, the remnant, the Messiah, the messianic kingdom, hopes of restoration, God's use of foreign nations, and many other ideas recur frequently in the messages of the prophet.

The Messenger and the Message—1:1–6:13

Nearly all the major themes throughout the Book of Isaiah are initially mentioned in the introduction. Unlike Jeremiah and Ezekiel, Isaiah records his call after he has portrayed the sinful and immortal conditions of the people to whom he is called to proclaim God's message.

Isaiah's basic indictment against the citizens of Judah is that they have broken their relationship with God: "They have forsaken the Lord; they have spurned the Holy One of Israel and turned their backs on him" (1:4). Instead of demonstrating love for their neighbors, they mistreat them. They oppress the poor and neglect widows and orphans. God is not pleased with their religious activities as long as injustice permeates the society. "Zion will be redeemed with justice" is the divine warning.

In direct contrast to this doom of Jerusalem, Isaiah holds forth the bright hope of restoration. In its restoration Zion will be the governing center of all nations, extending peace and righteousness throughout the world (2:1–4).

Admonishing his people to turn to God in obedience, Isaiah delineates the idolatry and sin that precipitate divine judgment. Hope and salvation await only those who put their trust in God. Isaiah illustrates his message with the parable of the vineyard, which has been labeled as one of the most perfect of its kind in the Bible. Israel, as God's vineyard, must be destroyed. In vain God has looked for fruits of righteousness (2:5–5:30).

Isaiah's call represents a fitting climax to this solemn charge against God's covenant people. God expresses his concern and love for his people by sending them a prophet to warn them of impending judgment. Hope is expressed in the assurance that a "holy seed" will remain when the land is depleted (6:1–13).

The Kingdom Prospects, Contemporary and Future—7:1–12:6

At the precise moment when Ahaz and his people are terrified by the prospect of an invasion by Pekah of Samaria and Rezin of Damascus, Isaiah comes with a message from God. Identifying Assyria as the real threat to Judah, the prophet warns Ahaz to trust in God for deliverance. Isaiah predicts that God will use the Assyrians as a rod to bring the ravages of war into Judah but will halt their plans to destroy Jerusalem. Ultimately Assyria will be subjected to God's judgment.

With godless Ahaz on the throne of David, a message of hope is delineated for the godly in the promise of a righteous ruler. These hopes are vested in the birth of a son, Immanuel (7:14). Identified as "Mighty God," or equal with God, a ruler will sit on David's throne and establish an everlasting kingdom (9:6–7). The ruler is of Davidic origin but has characteristics reaching beyond the human. He is divine in exercising righteous judgment through his omniscience and omnipotence. The knowledge of the Lord will extend throughout the world as absolute righteousness and universal peace extend from Zion (11:1–12:6).

Panorama of Nations—13:1–23:18

To the people of Judah and Jerusalem, who were conscious that they were God's chosen people, through whom Zion would be reestablished, the prophecies in 13:1–23:18 involving other nations were vitally significant. Although Assyria was Judah's number one problem in Isaian times, attention is primarily focused upon other prominent nations in these chapters.

The sovereignty and supremacy of God is basic throughout this entire passage. The title "Lord Almighty" (Lord of Hosts), occurs at least twenty-three times in these eleven chapters. Isaiah acknowledged God as such when he saw the "King the Lord Almighty" at the time of his call to the prophetic ministry (6:5). In the Lord Almighty, who used Assyria as a rod for judgment, rested the assurance of the establishment of an everlasting kingdom (9:7).

The purposes and plans of the Lord Almighty are frequently expressed throughout these messages concerning the nations. Judgment from God does not fall upon the nations by accident. Pride and arrogance are punished as God is ignored—regardless of its occurrence in heathen nations, Israel, Judah, or even in an individual such as Shebna the steward (22:15–25). No haughty individual or nation can escape.

Babylon with its king is singled out for judgment. Although the heyday of Babylonian power was still in the future, Isaiah predicted in the days of Hezekiah (39) that Babylon would be responsible for the captivity of Judah. For the people who survived, these chapters must have had special significance. Judgment awaited this kingdom that was temporarily used in the plan of God to purge Judah of its sin (586 B.C.). By that time the people had already witnessed the fall of Assyria, and this passage assured them that Babylon would likewise be judged.

The theme of Israel's restoration and kingdom hopes recurs throughout this passage. The assurance that Israel would have a worldwide kingdom with Zion as its capital, introduced in chapter 2, was a major theme in chapters 7–12, where special emphasis was given to the righteous ruler. Israel is still God's heritage (19:25) even though it is temporarily judged. Not only will the nation of Israel be restored (14:1–2), but aliens will be afforded a refuge there. Zion was founded by the Lord (14:32) and will be the recipient of gifts (18:7). While other nations and kingdoms are judged, a righteous ruler will be established on the Davidic throne (16:5). Such were the unparalleled promises of restoration repeatedly given to Israel for comfort and hope in periods when the Israelites were subjected to the judgments of God.

Israel in a World Setting—24:1–27:13

In 24:1–27:13 a righteous remnant in Israel is assured of survival and restoration. Jerusalem's doom had been clearly announced in chapter 1. In chapter 24 Jerusalem's ruin is portrayed with divine judgment extending worldwide. The wonders of the sky involving the sun and moon are associated with the disposal of those who oppose God and the establishment of the remnant in Zion in a universal kingdom without end.

Most appropriate is the song of the redeemed in 25:1–26:6. They respond with thanksgiving and praise as they rejoice in their salvation and enjoy the blessings of the Lord. Reproach, suffering, and shame will disappear as God wipes away all tears and eliminates death.

The prayer in 26:7–19 expresses the earnest desire of the people in times of great tribulation and suffering before they are regathered. Israel voices a hope while writhing in anguish and awaiting deliverance. Under the rule of the wicked as victims of prevailing unrighteousness, they express their faith and hope in God, appealing to him for divine intervention.

Deliverance is promised in the reply (26:20–27:13). Israel, God's vineyard, will once more be fruitful. Purged from their sin, the people will be gathered one by one as a remnant to worship the Lord in Jerusalem.

True and False Hopes in Zion—28:1–35:10.

Foreign alliances were a constant problem in Jerusalem during the days of Isaiah's ministry. Using political intrigue and diplomacy, the leaders of Judah hoped to ensure their survival as a nation by aligning themselves with the victor. Ahaz replaced his father Jotham on the Davidic throne when the pro-Assyrian party gained control in Judah in 735. He defied the warnings of Isaiah and made an alliance with Tiglath-pileser in the early years of his reign. Hezekiah, the next king, joined in an alliance with Edom, Moab, and Ashdod in resisting Assyria. This coalition anticipated support from Egypt, but Ashdod fell in 711 while the other nations offered tribute to the Assyrians to avert invasion.

Isaiah constantly warns against the folly of relying on foreign nations. He labels these alliances a "covenant with death." His advice is to place their faith in God, the true King of Israel. Whether it is Ahaz, the godless king, or Hezekiah, the godly ruler, who responds with friendly overtures to the Babylonian embassy, the prophet Isaiah constantly rebukes the leaders of Judah for depending upon other nations instead of looking to God for deliverance.

None of the chapters in this section is specifically dated. Since the alliance with Egypt receives such prominent consideration in chapters 30–31, this entire passage may be dated in the days of Hezekiah, when Judah had hopes of freeing itself from Assyrian domination. Chapters 28–29 could, however, refer to the alliance Ahaz made with Tiglath-pileser in 734 B.C. (cf. 7:1 ff.). Ahaz, instead of placing his faith in God, ignored Isaiah. The passing of the crisis of the Syro-Ephraimitic war and the apparently successful venture of a Judo-Assyrian union in 732, when Ahaz met Pul in Damascus, may have been the occasion for excessive celebration in Jerusalem. Ahaz and his associates, who were supported by priests and prophets in introducing Assyrian cult worship into Jerusalem, probably are the audience to whom Isaiah directs the stern words of rebuke recorded in chapters 28–29. Ahaz and his supporters undoubtedly concluded that the overwhelming scourge (28:15) of Assyrian invasion would not affect Judah because it made a treaty with this powerful nation. The warning is clear that both Assyria and Egypt will not aid Israel but will be overthrown (30:2, 31; 31:1–3, 8–9; 33:1). The antithesis to this warning against political alliances is the admonition to trust in God. The provision is made in Zion and the promises related to its establishment, so that those who exercise faith need not be anxious (28:16). God's plan for Zion as unfolded in these chapters affords a reasonable basis for the faith of the remnant who are willing to place their faith in God.

Divine assurance is given that God will again restore his people. Righteousness will prevail under the righteous king established in Zion. God's Spirit will be poured out; the prayers of the suffering and afflicted will not go unheeded; sinners will be judged; and the righteous remnant shall enjoy the blessings of the Lord (32–33).

Climactic is the gathering of all nations for a world judgment and the restoration of Zion (34–35). Nations guilty of offending Zion will be punished. The glory of Zion affords a hopeful contrast to the horrible judgments of God upon the sinful nations. The remnant returns to the promised land, which has been transformed from a wilderness into a land of plenty. God is bringing his righteous ones back to Zion to enjoy everlasting bliss.

Jerusalem's Judgment Delayed—36:1–39:8

Hezekiah is confronted with the ultimatum of surrendering Jerusalem to the Assyrians. Orally as well as by letter, Sennacherib harasses Hezekiah and his people about relying on Egypt or trusting in God. Hezekiah resorts to prayer. Isaiah boldly announces the safety of Jerusalem.

Hezekiah's serious illness apparently occurs during this period of international pressures. When Isaiah warns him to prepare for death, Hezekiah prays earnestly, receiving the assurance through Isaiah that his life will be extended for fifteen years. Deliverance from the Assyrian threat comes simultaneously. After Hezekiah's personal and national recovery, congratulations are extended to him by a Babylonian embassy sent by Merodach-baladan. Hezekiah's cordial reception of the Babylonians is the occasion for a significant prediction. Isaiah sternly warns that the treasures, which he had shown to the embassy, would be taken to Babylon in the future when Babylonian exile would be the lot of Jerusalem and Judah. This prediction was made seventy-five years before the days of Babylonian supremacy.

The Promise of Divine Deliverance—40:1–56:8

The promise of divine deliverance in this passage is not necessarily related to any particular incident in Hezekiah's time. Israel's exile is the perspective. As the ascendancy of wicked Manasseh to the Davidic throne dimmed the immediate prospect of the righteous remnant, Isaiah may well have been concerned with the needs of the people who would be taken into exile. For him the exile was certain.

Isaiah has an appropriate message of hope and comfort for those who anticipated Babylonian exile. Various themes are interwoven throughout this magnificent passage. With deliverance as the basic theme, not only are assurance and hope given but the provision for the accomplishment of these promises is vividly portrayed. In scope and magnitude as well as literary excellence, this great message is unsurpassed. Doubtless it was a source of comfort and blessing to the immediate audience of Isaiah as well as to those who went into Babylonian exile.

Deliverance and restoration are developed in three aspects: Israel's return from captivity under Cyrus, deliverance from sin, and the ultimate establishment of righteousness when Israel and foreigners will enjoy God's blessings forever. The scope of fulfillment covers a long period of time. Initial fulfillment comes in part with the return from captivity under Zerubbabel, Ezra, and Nehemiah; atonement for sin was historically unfolded in New Testament times; the establishment of the universal kingdom is still pending.

The guarantee of this great deliverance rested in a God who could accomplish all things. As captives looking for help, the people did not need a message of condemnation. Those who were subjected to the reality of the exile were conscious of their sinful past, for which they were suffering in accordance with Isaiah's warnings. To inspire faith and assure comfort Isaiah emphasizes the attributes and characteristics of God.

Suffering in exile, Israel is assured of comfort and pardon for its iniquity in preparation for the revelation of God's glory and rule in Zion. God, who is omnipotent, eternal, and infinite in wisdom, has created all things, directs and controls all the nations, has perfect knowledge and understanding of Israel in its suffering. Those who wait on God shall prosper. Faith in this Omnipotent One, who cannot be compared to idols, brings comfort and hope.

The servant theme is fascinating. Twenty times the word *servant* occurs—introduced in 41:8 and mentioned finally in 53:11. The initial use of the word *servant* is specifically identified with Israel chosen by God. However, Israel as God's servant is blind, deaf, and disobedient (42:19). God will not abandon her (44:1–2, 21). Jerusalem will be restored in the days of Cyrus, and Israel will be brought back from Babylonian captivity (48:20).

In 42:1–4 the ideal servant, also chosen by God, is introduced. Endowed with God's Spirit, this servant will establish justice in the earth and extend His law to distant lands—a mission in which Israel has failed.

Israel in its failure is in need of salvation. Atonement must be provided for Israel's sin, which God promises to blot out (44:22). To achieve this the ideal servant (49:1–6) has been chosen—not only to bring salvation to Israel but to be a light to the Gentiles. Ultimately the servant will have all nations prostrate before him (49:7 and 9:2–7). Before that can be accomplished, however, a sacrifice for sin must be provided. This servant who is to be exalted (52:13) must first make atonement for sin through suffering and death. Thus the ideal servant is identified with the suffering servant.

The suffering servant is dramatically portrayed in 52:13–53:12. It is significant that this servant is righteous and innocent. In contrast to Israel, who suffered for its sin in double measure (40:2), this servant suffers solely for the sins of others. Through vicarious suffering atonement is provided.

The climactic use of the word *servant* in 53:11 provides for the imputation of righteousness to those whose iniquities and sins are pardoned through this vicarious sacrifice. This servant does not waver or falter in the purpose for which he was chosen. Redemption is provided in his death. For bearing the sins of many, this servant is assured of a heritage and a spoil with the great and the strong.

Out of a fruitless and barren nation God will bring forth a prosperous people (54:1–17). Israel was temporarily judged and forsaken. As God prospered the ravager in bringing destruction and judgment, so he assures prosperity to his people, who are identified as his servants. They shall not be put to shame or defeated but will possess the nations and be established in righteousness.

The message of pardon and hope is issued to one and all (55: 1–56:8). Response to this gracious message brings life and blessing. As the wicked forsake their way and the unrighteous their thoughts they may enjoy the mercy of the Lord and obtain pardon from God through the atonement provided in the death of the suffering servant. The universal aspect is apparent in the fact that foreigners and eunuchs will conform to the ways of the Lord. Strange nations and people from afar will associate themselves with the Lord. The Temple will be a house of prayer for all peoples. The travail of soul by the righteous suffering servant will be satisfied in fruition—many individuals from all nations shall become the righteous servants of the Lord.

God's Universal Kingdom Established—56:9–66:24

The glory of Zion in its ultimate state has significance only as the individual has the assurance of participation—hence the comparison between the righteous and the unrighteous. Consequently Isaiah draws a sharp distinction between religious practice as Isaiah observed it and God's requirements (56:9–59:21).

Idolatry and oppression of the poor prevail among the laity as well as among the leaders, who are labeled as blind watchmen (56:9–57:13). They pray and fast as sin and iniquity, in the forms of social injustice, oppression, deeds of violence, and bloodshed, continue in open practice (58:1–5; 59:1–8). God is displeased with such things —judgment awaits them (cf. also chaps. 1–5).

By contrast, God delights in the individual who is contrite and humble in heart (57:15). Genuine fasting pleasing to God involves practice of the social gospel: loose the bands of wickedness, feed the hungry, and relieve the oppressed. These people are assured of answered prayer, guidance, and abundant blessings (58:9–11). Since national sins and iniquities have separated humanity from God, God will send a redeemer to Zion to vindicate the righteous (59:1–21).

The redeemer will establish Israel as the center and delight of all nations, so that Zion will be known as the city of the Lord. The glory of God will be displayed so universally that the sun and moon will be needed no more (60:1–22). In preparation for this coming revelation of God's glory, God will send his messenger to Zion—anointed by the Spirit of the Lord. He will proclaim the time of God's favor when brokenhearted may be healed, captives may be released, mourners may be comforted, and despondency may be turned into praise. Righteousness and praise will sprout forth before all nations (61:1–11). Ultimately Zion, which has been forsaken and desolate, will be vindicated and restored (62:1–63:6).

In 63:7–64:12 an appeal is made to God for help. On the basis of God's favor to Israel in the past, this prayer expresses a demand for divine intervention. God is blamed for causing the people to err and hardening their hearts, delivering them into the power of iniquity, and making them what they are. God's answer to their prayer (65:1–7) reflects his attitude toward the self-righteous who ignored him when he was available. They spurned his appeals and failed to turn to him in the day of mercy—their self-righteous appeal comes too late. The day of judgment is upon them, in contrast to the divine blessings for God's servants, mentioned seven times in 65:8–16.

Finally Isaiah describes the ultimate blessings for the righteous in Zion in terms of the new heaven and the new earth (65:17–66:24).

Jerusalem again is the focal point from which blessings extend universally, extending peace even to the animal world (cf. chaps. 2; 11–12; 24–27; 35). God, who has heaven as his throne and earth for his footstool, takes delight in individuals who are humble and contrite in spirit and tremble at God's word. Even though they have been subjected to scorn and ridicule, they will triumph in the establishment of Zion, while offenders will be condemned. As the unrighteous are judged it will be apparent that God's hand is upon his servants. The redeemed from all nations share in the blessings of Zion, while those who rebelled are subjected to endless punishment.

Chapter 13

EXILE AND RESTORATION HOPES

The destruction of Jerusalem was the greatest judgment upon the nation of Israel in Old Testament times. Warning his people for forty years about the impending doom of the Davidic kingdom, Jeremiah lived through the hectic years of Babylonian invasions. He personally witnessed the razing of Jerusalem with its temple in 586 B.C. The same warning was given by Ezekiel beginning in 593 B.C. to the exiles in the environs of Babylon.

Warning of Impending Judgment—Jeremiah and Lamentations

Jeremiah has much to say to his own generation as he passionately warns them of impending doom, especially after Josiah's death. Compared with Isaiah he devotes relatively little space to future hopes of restoration. He concentrates on current problems in an effort to turn his generations God-ward. A man with a vital message during the last forty years of Judah's existence as a kingdom, Jeremiah relates more of his personal experience than any other prophet in Old Testament times.

Born in Anathoth, three miles northeast of Judah's capital, Jeremiah became conversant with the currents that swept through Jerusalem. He was called to the prophetic ministry around 627 B.C. when twenty-year-old Josiah was leading Judah in a nationwide reformation. Little is indicated in the scriptural record concerning Jeremiah's activities during the first eighteen years of his ministry (627–609

B.C.). The simple statement that he mourned Josiah's death in 609 (2 Chron. 35:25) and the common interest of prophet and king warrant the conclusion that he actively supported Josiah's reformation.

The years 609–586 B.C. were most hectic for Jeremiah as politically the sun was setting on Judah's national existence and international conflicts brought shadows of extinction that ultimately left Jerusalem in ruins. In religious matters most of the evils eliminated by Josiah returned under Jehoahaz, there was once again idolatry in Jerusalem. The year 605 marked the beginning of Babylonian captivity for some citizens of Jerusalem, while Jehoiakim pledged allegiance to the invading Babylonians. In 597 King Jehoiachin, with approximately ten-thousand Jews, was taken into exile.

With the remaining lower classes of people controlling the government under their puppet king Zedekiah, the prophet Jeremiah continued his ministry. In the religious and political struggle he faced more opposition and encountered more enemies than any other Old Testament prophet. He was arrested in the Temple court, beaten, and placed in the stocks for the right (19–20). Priests and prophets rose en masse against him and demanded his execution (26). He had a personal encounter with the false prophet Hananiah (28). Other false prophets were active in Jerusalem as well as in Babylon opposing Jeremiah and his message (29). Even the people of Jeremiah's hometown Anathoth rose against him; they threatened to kill him unless he stopped prophesying (11:21–23). Civil rulers he encountered reported him to Jehoiakim, who blatantly defied Jeremiah's warning and burned his scroll (36).

Under Zedekiah's weak rule Jeremiah suffered the consequences of vacillating policies (597–586). At times Zedekiah sought the prophet's advice, but often Jeremiah was subject to arrest and imprisonment and once was even thrown into a cistern where he was left to sink in the mire. Rescued by Ebed-melech, an Ethiopian eunuch, he was restored to the court of the guard, where Zedekiah had one more interview with him on the eve of Jerusalem's fall to the Babylonian invaders (34–39).

Jeremiah had relatively few friends during the days of Jehoiakim and Zedekiah. Most loyal and devoted was Baruch, who served as the prophet's secretary. He recorded Jeremiah's messages and read them in the Temple court (36:6), served as business manager when Jeremiah was in prison (32:9-14), and finally accompanied his master to Egypt. Among the community leaders who saved Jeremiah from execution at the demands of the priests and prophets (26:16-24) were the princes led by Ahikam.

Through times of opposition and suffering Jeremiah experienced deep inner conflict. Penetrating grief pierced his soul as he realized that his calloused people were indifferent to warnings and would be subjected to God's terrible judgment. They did not believe Jeremiah's warning that the Temple would be destroyed and continued in their idolatry and social evils (7-8). This was the cause of his weeping day and night—not the personal suffering he had to endure (9:1). Consequently, the ascription of "weeping prophet" to Jeremiah denotes strength and courage and willingness to face the bitter realities of coming judgment alongside his people.

Throughout his ministry Jeremiah could not escape the God-given conviction that he was God's messenger. True to human experience, he sank to the depths of despondency in times of persecution, cursing the day he was born (20). When remaining silent to avoid the persecution, the word of God became a burning fire within that compelled him to continue in the prophetic ministry. Continually he experienced the divine sustenance promised him in chapter 1. Often threatened and on the brink of death, in the pressures of life Jeremiah was providentially sustained as a living witness for God in the fading years of Judah's national life.

Jeremiah survived the destruction of Jerusalem and was favorably treated by the conquering Babylonians. Given the choice, Jeremiah did not join the Jews who were taken into exile but remained with those who were left in Judah. When their homeless and discouraged leaders appealed to Jeremiah to ascertain the Lord's will for them, he informed them that they should remain in Palestine in order to enjoy God's blessings. But the people deliberately disobeyed and migrated to Egypt, taking the aged prophet with them. Bypassing the city of Jerusalem on his way to Egypt, Jeremiah must have taken one last look at the ruins of his beloved city, which for over four centuries had represented the glory and pride of his nation Israel.

Out of this experience Jeremiah very likely wrote the Book of Lamentations, contrasting Israel's desolation with its former glory and confessing that the sins of his people have precipitated this divine judgment. In this reality of despair and hopelessness he remembers that "the Lord's great love" and "his compassions" are "new every morning" (2:22-23). Out of a broken heart, crushed and overwhelmed with sorrow, Jeremiah makes his plaintive appeal to the God who reigns forever, imploring him to restore his own. In confession of sin and an implicit faith in God rests his final appeal for mercy and restoration.

In the Book of Jeremiah the dated events and messages are not in chronological order. Many passages are not dated at all. Consequently it is difficult to arrange the contents of this book in chronological order with absolute certainty. The following outline may be helpful for further study:

The prophet and his people	1:1-18:23
The prophet and the leaders	19:1-29:32
The promise of restoration	30:1-33:36
Disintegration of the kingdom	34:1-39:18
The migration to Egypt	40:1-45:5
Prophecies concerning nations and cities	46:1-51:64
Appendix or conclusion	52:1-34.

Divine Assurance for the Exiles—Ezekiel

At the time of Ezekiel's birth (622/21 B.C.) Jerusalem was astir with the greatest celebration of the Passover in centuries as Josiah's kingdom temporarily responded to nationwide reforms. Not only did optimism prevail religiously, but the fading influence of Assyrian domination in Palestine gave rise to brighter prospects politically.

Ashurbanipal, whose reign in Assyria ended about 630 B.C., had not been succeeded by kings powerful enough to resist Median and Babylonian advances. The news of Nineveh's fall in 612 undoubtedly relieved Judah of the fear that Assyrian armies would ever again threaten its independence.

With religious activities flourishing in the Temple under royal support, Ezekiel, a member of the priestly family, must have enjoyed pleasant associations with the devout people of Judah. His home may have been located on the eastern wall of Jerusalem, so that the outer courts were his playground and the adjoining precincts of the Temple classrooms for his formal training and education. These early years under the shadows of Solomon's Temple acquainted him with every detail of this magnificent edifice as well as the rituals of daily ministration. In addition Ezekiel may have assisted his father and other priests during his boyhood years. Consequently, when he was taken to Babylon he had vivid memories of the Temple and its place in the life of his people.

As a boy of nine Ezekiel may not have been impressed with the news of Nineveh's fall, but three years later the sudden death and burial of King Josiah must have made an indelible impression upon him—he was still in his formative years. This was followed by the coronation of Jehoahaz, his captivity three months later, and the coronation of Jehoiakim as an Egyptian vassal. In 605 B.C. Ezekiel must have considered himself fortunate to escape being included with Daniel and others who were taken as hostages to Babylon.

Even though he never mentions Jeremiah, it is unlikely that Ezekiel was unaware of the message of this prophet who was so well known in Jerusalem. Surely Ezekiel had witnessed the mob reaction to Jeremiah's Temple sermon (Jer. 26) when the princes refused to allow the execution of Jeremiah by the people and their religious leaders. Could he possibly have been among the priests who tried to seize Jeremiah? Perhaps he was puzzled by the fact that Jehoiakim had the prophet Uriah executed and boldly burned the scroll of Jeremiah without being subjected to immediate judgment.

In 597 B.C. Ezekiel, as a young man of twenty-five, was taken to Babylonian exile with ten thousand of the leading citizens of Jerusalem, including king Jehoiachin. With his fellow exiles he settled on the banks of the Kebar River not far from Babylon. In spite of Nebuchadnezzar's increase in dominion and power, the exiles were optimistic about an early return to their native land. Reports from Jerusalem, where Hananiah predicted that the Babylonian yoke would be broken in two years (Jer. 28:1 ff.), encouraged them to hope for a speedy return. When Jeremiah advised them by letter that they should settle down and prepare for a seventy-year exile, the false prophets become more active (Jer. 29). Shemaiah wrote back to Jerusalem, charging Jeremiah with the responsibility for their captivity and demanding that he be confined to the stocks. In a public letter to the exiles Jeremiah in turn identified Shemaiah as a false prophet. Apparently the activity of the false prophets became so serious that two of their leaders, Ahab and Zedekiah, were executed.

In 593 B.C. Ezekiel was divinely commissioned to be a spokesman for God to his fellow exiles. In opposition to the false prophets, he was to warn the people that Jerusalem was doomed for destruction—the same message that Jeremiah proclaimed in Judah. In his divine call he has a fantastic vision of God's glory (1:1–3:21) and is made conscious of the presence of God, which he normally associated with the Temple in Jerusalem. Commissioned as a watchman for the house of Israel he is charged with the responsibility to warn them. If they perish in spite of his warning he is not guilty.

By symbolic action Ezekiel portrays the pending fate of Jerusalem (3:22–7:27). Idolatry is the reason for this judgment. Most sobering is the vision in which Ezekiel sees the idolatrous condition prevailing in the shadows of the Temple (8:1–11:25). With the elders participating in idol worship, the women weeping for Tammuz the god of vegetation, and seventy-five men in the inner court worshiping the sun, God is provoked to wrath. The glory of God abandons the Temple, and executioners are sent, beginning at the Temple, to mete out divine judgment. Mercy, however, precedes judgment as a man dressed in linen marks all individuals who deplore the idolatry for exclusion from execution. Ezekiel then shares this vision with the exiles.

Ezekiel enacts before his Israelite audience in symbolic action the bitter experiences awaiting the residents in Jerusalem. He charges the religious leaders with deluding the people by assuring them of peace, when the wrath of God is awaiting them. Jerusalem is so sinful that no one can save it from destruction. Even if Noah, Daniel, or Job were in Jerusalem God would not spare the city (12:1–15:8).

In allegorical language Ezekiel portrays the corruption of Israelite religion. Helpless as a newborn babe, Israel was nurtured by God. Now Israel is as deliberate in its apostasy as a harlot is in her sinful ways. They will be punished for their sins. Although the exile was a place of corporate suffering Ezekiel draws a line of demarcation—the unrighteous perish, but the righteous shall live. Each individual ultimately is responsible to God (16:1–19:14).

In 591, with the elders before him, Ezekiel once more reviews Israel's history (20:1–23:49). The sin of foreign alliances, which involved recognition of pagan gods, constituted a serious offense against God. The fall of Samaria (722 B.C.) should have been a warning to Judah. Now the cup of God's wrath is at hand.

On the very same day (January 15, 588 B.C.) that the Babylonian armies surrounded Jerusalem, Ezekiel was given another message (24:1–24). While he dramatically portrays the complete destruction of Jerusalem, Ezekiel's wife dies. As a significant sign to his audience Ezekiel is commanded not to mourn publicly. Neither are the people to mourn when they receive the news that the Temple in Jerusalem has been destroyed.

Most of Ezekiel's prophecies against foreign nations (25:1–32:32) occur during the period of Nebuchadnezzar's siege of Jerusalem, 588–586 B.C. These nations, like Judah, will also come under God's judgment.

In January, 586 B.C., a fugitive from Jerusalem reports to Ezekiel and the exiles that the city has actually capitulated to the Babylonian army. God now bids Ezekiel to speak again, reminding him that he is a watchmen to the house of Israel (33:1–33). In a message of hope he compares the unfaithfulness of the shepherds of Israel with the faithfulness of God, who is portrayed as the true Shepherd of Israel (34:1–31). The thesis of Israel's restoration is developed in contrast to the antithesis of Edom's destruction (35:1–36:38). Gathering Israel from all nations, God will transform them, impart to them a new heart and a new spirit, and purify them in preparation for being his people.

Dim were the prospects for restoration from the human perspective. Led by the Spirit of the Lord into the midst of a valley filled with dry bones, Ezekiel sees these bones take on life. This revival of dead bones signifies the restoration of the whole house of Israel—including both the Northern and the Southern Kingdom. They will be reunited under "my servant David" (37:1–28). In its own land Israel will be challenged by Gog, of the land of Magog, leading massive invading armies from the north. This, however will be a day of divine vindication. The forces of nature, in the form of earthquake, rain, hail, fire, and brimstone, will be released against the invaders. Gathering the spoils of war, Israel will dwell safely in their own land with none to make them afraid (38:1–39:29).

In 573 B.C. Ezekiel has another vision (40:1–48:35). The focal point is the Temple in Jerusalem. He sees the glory of God return to the Temple, signifying that God is establishing his eternal dwelling place with his people. The land of Canaan is allotted to the Israelites, and Jerusalem is identified as "The Lord is there."

Israel's Ultimate Prospects—Daniel

Daniel was probably in his teens when he was taken as a hostage from Jerusalem to Babylon in 605 B.C. There he served in the Babylonian court under Nebuchadnezzar and Belshazzar, and under Darius after the Persians conquered the city of Babylon in 539 B.C.

Daniel and his three friends—Hananiah, Mishael, and Azariah—together with other Jewish youths, were selected for special training in the royal college. Facing the problem of defilement when offered the lavish menu of the heathen court, Daniel, as spokesman for the group, courageously but courteously appealed to the chief steward to provide them with a menu of their own choice on a ten-day trial basis. At the end of this period the steward was pleased to find Daniel and his friends in better health than their fellow trainees. Before long it was obvious that these Hebrew youths were endowed with extraordinary skill and wisdom. When interviewed by the king, Daniel and his friends received highest honors and were recognized as far superior to all the other wise men at the royal court (1:1–21).

The affinity of religion and politics must have made an indelible impression on Daniel. At various times during the accession year of Nebuchadnezzar, which reached its climax in the celebration of the New Year's Day festival, the king acknowledged the gods Nabu and Marduk as he led them in public procession, ending at the Akitu temple. Daniel may have been perplexed when he saw Nebuchadnezzar extend his conquests in the name of these heathen gods.

In the second year of his reign Nebuchadnezzar had a perplexing dream. Called before the king, Daniel not only related to him his dream but also gave its interpretation. He identified Nebuchadnezzar as the head of gold in this dream's colossal image, informing him that God had given him this great empire. Eventually God will establish a kingdom that shall never be destroyed. Hearing this, Nebuchadnezzar made Daniel ruler over the province of Babylon and gave him the highest position among all wise men (2:1–49).

Daniel must have observed with great concern, though without personal involvement, the triumphant march of the Babylonians, especially as it brought King Jehoiachin and ten-thousand Jews from Jerusalem captive to Babylonia in 597 B.C. This was followed by tragedy when Zedekiah rebelled and precipitated the destruction of Jerusalem and the reduction of the Temple to ashes in 586 B.C. Probably it was during this time that Nebuchadnezzar erected a great image on the plains of Dura. Under threat of death, Daniel's three friends refused to worship in prostration. Arrested and brought before the king, they expressed their faith in God. When they were miraculously spared in the fiery furnace Nebuchadnezzar acknowledged that their God had delivered them (3:1-30).

Probably during the last two decades of his reign, which ended in 562 B.C., Nebuchadnezzar was subjected to an experience of humiliation and restoration (4:1-37). Again Daniel is involved. The king is warned through a dream that the Most High has decreed that he will be demoted unless he rights his ways. It appears that Nebuchadnezzar ignores this warning. Boasting about making Babylon the most significant capital of ancient times, he is suddenly smitten with lycanthropy in divine judgment, deprived of his kingdom, and relegated to life among the beasts for a period designated as "seven times." When his reason returns to him, he is reinstated as king. In an official proclamation he acknowledges that the Most High is omnipotent and confesses that the King of heaven is just and right.

In the first year of Belshazzar's reign (about twelve years later, ca. 550 B.C.), Daniel has a vision of beasts representing successive kingdoms, which culminate in the everlasting kingdom ruled by the Most High and his people (7:1-28). In 547 B.C. Daniel has another vision, in which he is specifically informed that Medo-Persia and Greece will follow as successive kingdoms after Babylon (8:1-28).

In 539 B.C. Daniel is called before Belshazzar in a large banquet hall to interpret a divinely written message on the wall. There Daniel warns the king on the eve of his death that his kingdom will be given to the Medes and Persians. Babylon was conquered that night (5:1-30).

Daniel was given extensive responsibility under Darius, who was the Median ruler in Babylon under Cyrus (5:31; 6:28; cf. 1:21). As an able and competent administrator, he is tested in his devotion and worship of God when he is more than seventy years old. When his two fellow administrators succeed in having him placed in the lion's den, Daniel's life is miraculously spared. Subsequently Darius issues a decree "that in every part of my kingdom people must fear and reverence the God of Daniel" (6:1-28).

Daniel's deep-seated concern for his people is expressed in his prayer after reading God's word given to Jeremiah that Jerusalem would be restored (9:1–27; cf Jer. 25:11 and 29:10). Through the divine interpretation of the "seventy sevens," Daniel is assured that his nation, for whom he is praying, has a definite place in God's plan. Undoubtedly he is greatly encouraged as Cyrus, soon after he subdues Babylon, issues a proclamation encouraging Jews to return to their own land.

The final revelation came to Daniel in the third year of Cyrus (10:1–12:13). By now the statesman-prophet was well established in the Medo-Persian government. If Daniel was in his teens when taken captive, he would now be in his eighties. From the standpoint of age and responsibilities in government, it is not likely that he seriously considered joining the exodus of Jews returning to Jerusalem. Nevertheless he had a genuine interest in the welfare and future hopes of his people. In response to this divine revelation of the future, he expresses his concern about his people. He is assured that Michael, the prince of Israel, will arise to deliver them. Those who are wise and turn to righteousness will be the participants in God's blessings and everlasting life. Even though the coming events are not clear to Daniel, he is promised rest and an allotted place at the end of time. With this personal hope and the assurance that his people will ultimately triumph, Daniel is instructed to seal his book.

Chapter 14

MINOR PROPHETS—THE TWELVE

Due to their brevity the writings of the twelve minor prophets were all kept on one large scroll as early as the second century B.C. In the Greek version of the Old Testament they became known as the twelve-prophet book. As a guide for reading these with a better understanding, consider the following groupings: In times of prosperity (Jonah, Amos, and Hosea), warnings to Judah (Joel, Micah, and Zephaniah), foreign nations in prophecy (Obadiah, Nahum, and Habakkuk), beyond the exile (Haggai, Zechariah, and Malachi).

In Times of Prosperity

Jonah, Amos, and Hosea

Jonah, whose life and ministry may be placed in the early eighth century B.C., came from the village of Gath Hepher, about three miles northeast of Nazareth. He predicted that Jeroboam II (793–753 B.C.) would restore to Israel the territory from the Dead Sea in the south to Hamath in the north (2 Kings 14:25). This popular message may have been most welcome for the Israelites, who had been subjected to the oppressive occupation of this territory under Hazael of Damascus, who died about 798 B.C. There is no indication that Jonah had a message of warning or judgment to deliver the Israelites.

Jonah's sermon to the Ninevites was anything but cajolery. Judgment and doom for this foreign city were summed up in the theme, "Forty more days and Nineveh will be destroyed." The immediate response was, "The Ninevites believed God. They declared a fast, and all of them, from the greatest to the least, put on sackcloth." With the king and his people in penitence, the divine judgment upon this great city was postponed at least half a century until 612 B.C., when it was destroyed by the Medo-Babylonian armies. The following is a brief analytic outline:

Jonah's round-trip westward excursion	1:1–2:10
A successful preaching mission	3:1–10
The lesson for Jonah	4:1–11

Amos, a herdsman and prophet, came to the Northern Kingdom from Tekoa, located about five miles south of Bethlehem. His message reflects the luxury and ease of Israel during Jeroboam's reign. Boldly he indicts the Israelites for their moral corruption, selfish luxury, and oppression of the poor as the wealthy ruthlessly accumulate more riches. In simple but forceful language he boldly denounces the evils that permeated the social, economic, and political life of Israel. In religion rituals were no substitute for righteousness, without which the nation of Israel could not escape the judgment of a righteous God. Exile for Israel was imminent. Amos concludes with a message of hope, assuring the Israelites of the restoration of the kingdom under the Davidic dynasty. The following outline may be used for further study:

Introduction and denunciation of the nations	1:1–2:16
God's charge against Israel expanded	3:1–6:14
God's plan for Israel	7:1–9:15

Hosea, was outstanding as a messenger of God's love during the last few decades of the disintegration of the Northern Kingdom, before Samaria was conquered by the Assyrians in 722 B.C. With civil strife in Samaria after Jeroboam's death in 753, the threat to Israel's existence as a kingdom became more ominous with the reign of Tiglath-pileser (745–727).

During his long ministry Hosea shared the plight of his people in a tottering kingdom. With compassion and love for his fellow human beings, he manifested a sensitive response to the needs of Israel in its sinful condition. Out of his personal experience he expressed in tones of pathos the love of God for a people who failed to respond to his goodness. The following outline is based on an analysis of his message:

Hosea's marriage and its application to Israel	1:1–3:5
God's charges against Ephraim	4:1–6:3
God's decision to punish Ephraim	6:4–10:15
God's resolution in judgment and mercy	11:1–14:9

Warnings to Judah

Joel, Micah, and Zephaniah

Joel the prophet is unknown to us beyond the limits of his book. Based on internal evidence it is reasonable to date him during the early reign of Joash, who was crowned king at the age of seven (ca. 830 B.C.). Jehoiada, the high priest and uncle of Joash, exercised a controlling influence as the elders and priests bore the responsibility of national leadership while Judah recovered from the reign of terror under Athaliah. The following outline shows the development of Joel's message:

The locust plague	1:1–12
Admonition and intercession	1:13–20
Warning and exhortation	2:1–17
God's response and promise	2:18–32
Universal judgment and blessing	3:1–21.

Micah was a reformer in the turbulent times when the sun was setting on Judah's era of prosperity and international prestige in the wake of Uzziah's death in 740 B.C. Beginning in 745 B.C. Assyria extended its domination into Syria and Israel, and into Judah by the end of that century. He predicts the fall of Samaria as well as the destruction of Jerusalem, fearlessly pointing out the prevailing evils. Like Amos he does not hesitate to denounce the landlords and rulers for oppressing the poor. With Isaiah he announces the coming doom as well as the hopes of restoration for Zion and the chosen nation. Micah concludes with a prayer of praise. No wonder the prophet exclaims, "Who is a God like you, who pardons sin and forgives the transgression of the remnant of his inheritance?" The following outline may serve as an introduction to a more detailed consideration of Micah's message:

Charges against Samaria and Jerusalem	1:1–16
The leaders condemned	2:1–3:12
Restoration of Zion	4:1–5:1
The shepherd-king from Bethlehem	5:2–15
Contemporary versus future conditions	6:1–7:20.

Zephaniah, possibly a descendant of Hezekiah and a resident of Jerusalem, probably delivered his message in the early part of Josiah's reign. Like a blaring trumpet he raises his voice to shock the complacent citizens of Judah, announcing that the day of the Lord is at hand. It is a day of judgment. Besides indicting Judah for gross idolatry and bloodshed, Zephaniah points up the portentous stirrings in the Tigris-Euphrates area. With doom so near, the prophet not only sets forth the immediate implications but also warns of the final time of reckoning in the day of the Lord. In a brief message he covers the scope of judgments extending to the entire world:

The impending doom of Jerusalem	1:1–18
The scope of God's judgment	2:1–3:8
Restoration and blessing	3:9–20

Foreign Nations in Prophecy

Obadiah, Nahum, and Habakkuk

Obadiah, whose book is the shortest in the Old Testament, is unknown beyond his oracle, which offers no information about him beyond his name. Among all the prophetical books Obadiah is the most difficult to date; suggested dates range from the time of Jehoshaphat (848–841 B.C.) to 585, shortly after the destruction of Jerusalem. In twenty-one verses he denounces Edom for taking pride in its impregnable rock fortress (1–9) and points out how they gloated in the days of Jerusalem's calamity and even surrendered fugitives to the enemy, making them guilty of flagrant injustice (10–14). The day of the Lord will be a reckoning day for all nations, especially Edom (15–16). Mount Esau, once representative of the pride and haughtiness of the Edomites, will be ruled from Mount Zion (17–21).

Nahum lived after the conquest of Thebes by the Assyrians in 561 B.C. and before the destruction of Nineveh by the Medes and Babylonians in 612 B.C. Although his hometown, Elkosh, has never been identified with certainty, it is likely that he was a citizen of Judah. Known to him were the hardships that Judah endured during the century of Assyrian domination when they took Manasseh the king of Judah into exile and when Ashurbanipal marched his armies some five hundred miles up the Nile to Thebes.

The fate of Nineveh is the theme of his message. In his sovereignty and omnipotence God allows the wicked, his enemies, to continue because he is slow to anger. In due time God's vengeance will be released in the destruction of Nineveh. Vividly Nahum portrays the siege, conquest, plunder, and utter ruination of this proud city of the Assyrians who plagued Jerusalem. Addressing Nineveh, he asks, "Are you better than Thebes?" Like Thebes, which fell under the assault of the Assyrian armies, so Nineveh will be crushed. Everyone will rejoice in its destruction. Note in the following outline the leading themes of his message:

The majesty of God in judgment and mercy	1:1-14
Nineveh's siege and destruction	1:15-2:13
The reason for Nineveh's fall	3:1-19

Habakkuk very likely witnessed the decline and fall of the Assyrian empire during his lifetime. The fall of Nineveh in 612 B.C. may have occurred before Habakkuk made his appearance as a spokesman for God. Concerned about the apostasy, violence, and strife in Judah, the prophet is informed that God will send the Chaldeans in judgment. In his dialogue with God Habakkuk questions God's use of a godless nation to punish his own people:

Why does God allow violence?	1:1-4
God arouses the Chaldeans to punish Judah	1:5-11
Why should the wicked punish the upright?	1:12-2:1
The righteous live by faith and hope	2:2-4
Denunciation of the unrighteous	2:5-20
A psalm of praise	3:1-19

Beyond the Exile

Haggai, Zechariah, and Malachi

Haggai, very likely born in Babylon, returned in the migration of Jewish exiles to Jerusalem in 539-538 B.C. The enthusiasm with which the Jews laid the foundation for rebuilding the Temple was soon squelched by the Samaritans. For almost two decades they diverted their efforts to building their own houses. Beginning in late August of 520 B.C., Haggai delivered four messages to his people before the end of the year, stimulating the Jews to resume their efforts in rebuilding the Temple (Ezra 5:1-2; 6:14). The following outline is based on the four oracles:

Rebuke of the people and their response	1:1-15
The greater glory of the new Temple	2:1-9
An assurance of blessing	2:10-19
A personal message	2:20-23.

Zechariah began his ministry after Haggai's second message, when Jerusalem was buzzing with activity and excitement, and lent further inspiration to the struggling band of Jews. Very likely he was of the priestly lineage of Iddo and a young man when he began his ministry in 520 B.C. (cf. Neh. 12:1, 4, 16). Chapters 1-8 are definitely related to the time of rebuilding the Temple (520-515 B.C.). The remainder of his book may reasonably be dated in the latter years of his life. The following is an analytic outline of the Book of Zechariah:

The call of repentance	1:1-6
The night visions	1:7-6:8
The coronation of Joshua	6:9-15
The problem of fasting	7:1-8:23
The shepherd-king	9:1-11:17
The universal ruler	12:1-14:21

Warning his people not to ignore God as their forefathers had done, Zechariah admonishes them to turn to God in repentance. Based on a series of eight visions, Zechariah brings vital encouragement to his people as they engage in their noble struggle to rebuild the Temple during those anxious years. Divine assurance is given that the Jerusalem Temple will be restored (1:7-17). The nations responsible for the dispersion of the Jews will be destroyed (1:18-21). God will terrify the nations, regathering his people to dwell among them in Jerusalem, which will be expanded beyond its walls (2:1-13). In another vision the high priest Joshua is clothed in clean raiment, assuring the Jews that he can acceptably represent them before God (3:1-10). In the vision of the golden candlestick, assurance came to Zerubbabel that God by his Spirit would enable him to complete the rebuilding of the Temple (4:1-14). Dramatic indeed is the vision of the flying scroll announcing the curse sent from the Lord to consume all the guilty in the land (5:1-4). Removal of wickedness is portrayed as a woman is taken to Babylon in a measuring basket (5:5-11). In the final vision chariots depart to the four points of the compass to patrol the earth, assuring the Jews that the Lord of all the earth exercises universal control as he did in the opening vision through the four horsemen (6:1–8).

Doubtless there were many who wondered how long they could continue their building program. They had been stopped once; it could happen again. The problem of their immediate future, dependent as it was on the decree of the Persian king, disturbed the Jewish community more than a little. Climactic as well as predictive was Zechariah's symbolic act crowning Joshua as high priest, combining royalty and priesthood (6:9–15). Soon word came from Darius, the Persian king, nullifying the attempt of their enemies to hinder construction and ordering them to aid the Jews with material supplies and revenue (Ezra 6:6–15).

After two years pass in the building program, a delegation from Bethel comes to Jerusalem with an inquiry concerning fasting. Reassuring them once more that God will restore Jerusalem, Zechariah advises them that fasting should be changed into sessions of joy (7:1–8:23).

In a later message he announces the prospects that await Jerusalem. Humble and lowly in appearance, a righteous king will come to Zion to bring salvation. Ultimately he will establish universal peace as he rescues Ephraim and Judah from among the nations (9:1–10:12). Although abandoned to the nations by worthless shepherds (11:1–17) Israel has a place in God's plan. Jerusalem will be made "an immovable rock for all the nations. All who try to move it will injure themselves." All nations will be defeated, Jerusalem will be secure, and "the Lord will be king over the whole earth" (12:1–14:21).

Malachi, probably in the days of Nehemiah, came with a final prophetic warning in Old Testament times. He reminds them that as God's favored people they do not revere God, showing their disrespect by bringing imperfect or stolen animals in sacrifice (1:1–14). Priests are singled out for retribution (2:1–9). The people have desecrated "the sanctuary the Lord loves" by bringing in foreign wives with their idols (2:10–16). The charges against apostate Jews are sorcery, adultery, false swearing, failure to tithe, and social injustice toward hirelings, widows, orphans, and strangers (2:17–3:15).

But those who fear the Lord and revere his name are God's special possession, entered in God's "scroll of remembrance." They are designated for salvation. In contrast, those who do not serve God await the day of God's wrath (3:16–4:6). This terrible day will be preceded by a period of mercy ushered in with the coming of Elijah. Predictive in import, the name "Elijah" suggested a time of revival through a God-sent individual. Such a one had already been promised (3:1). Some four centuries later this messenger was identified (Matt. 11:10, 14).

APPENDIX

APPENDIX / 177

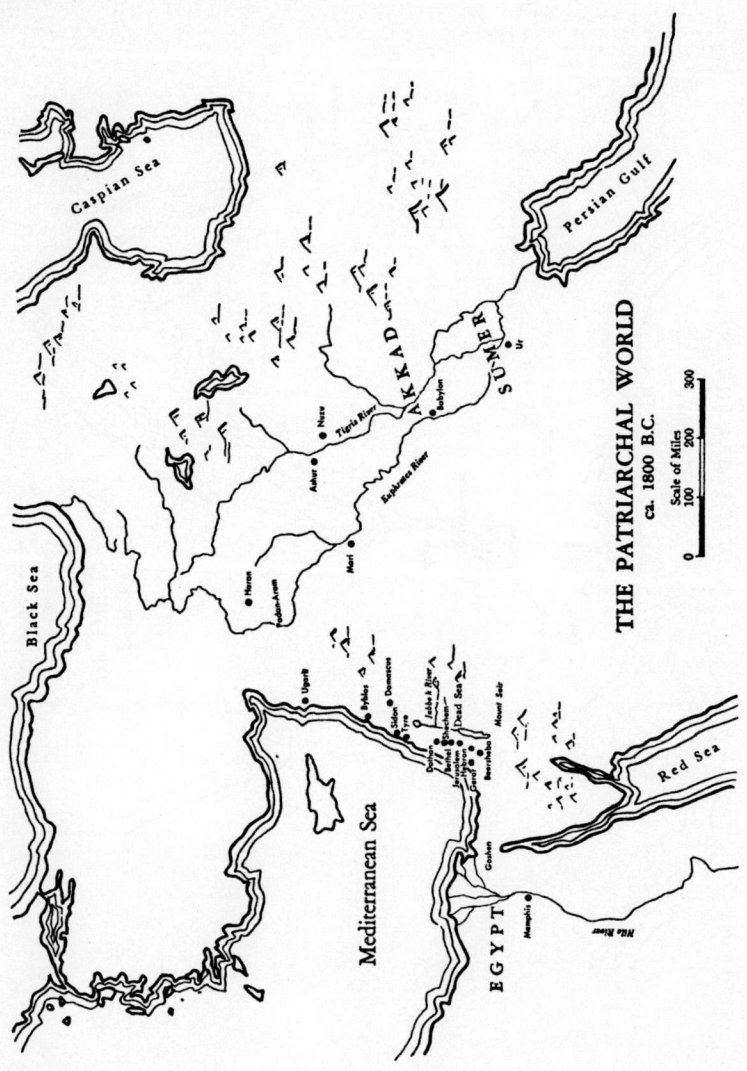

Figure 1

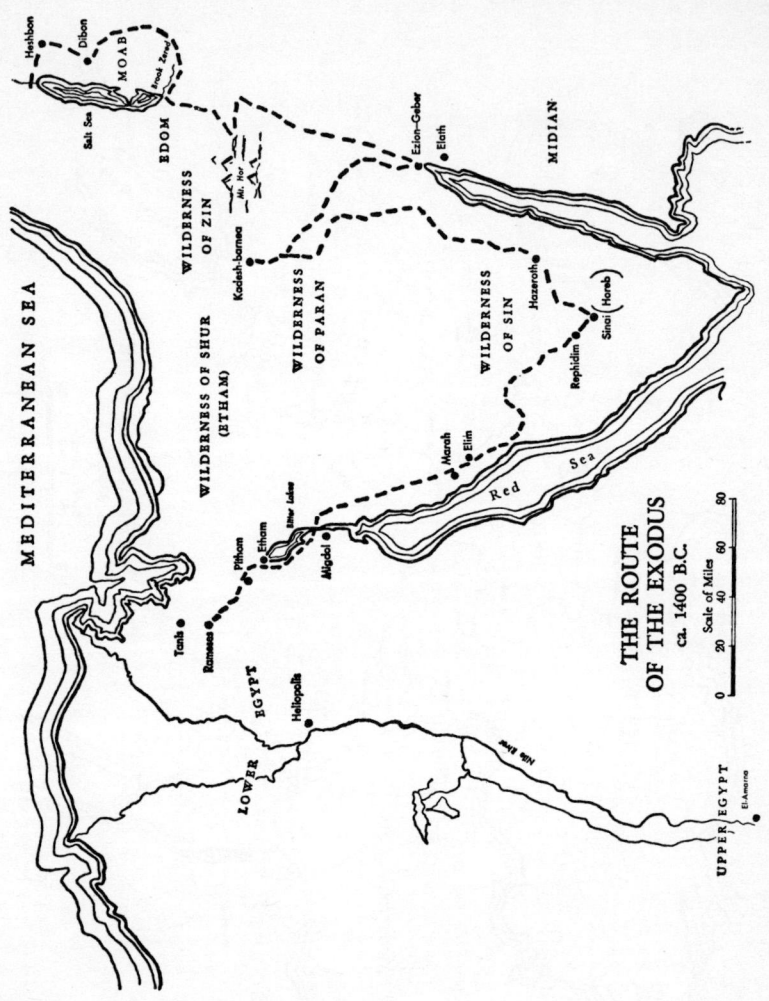

Figure 2

THE ANNUAL CALENDAR

Sacred year	Hebrew months	Civil year	Modern equivalent	Babylonian month	Farm season
1	Abib (Nisan) 1—New Moon 14—Passover 15—Sabbath—holy convocation 16—week of unleavened bread 21—holy convocation	7	March/April	Nisanu	later spring rain beginning of barley harvest
2	Iyyar (Ziv) 1—New Moon	8	April/May	Aiaru	barley harvest
3	Sivan 1—New Moon 6–7 Feast of Weeks	9	May/June	Simanu	wheat harvest
4	Tammuz 1—New Moon	10	June/July	Duzu	
5	Ab 1—New Moon	11	July/Aug.	Abu	figs and olives ripen
6	Elul 1—New Moon	12	Aug./Sept.	Ululu	vintage season
7	Tishri (Ethanim) 1—New Moon New Year's Day Feast of Trumpets 10—Day of Atonement 15–22 Feast of Tabernacles	1	Sept./Oct.	Tashritu	former early rains plowing time
8	Heshvan 1—New Moon	2	Oct./Nov.	Arahsamnu	seeding time for wheat and barley
9	Kislev (Chislev) 1—New Moon	3	Nov./Dec.	Kislimu	
10	Tebeth	4	Dec./Jan.	Tebetu	
11	Shebat	5	Jan./Feb.	Shabatu	
12	Adar	6	Feb./March	Addaru	almond trees blossom

Figure 3

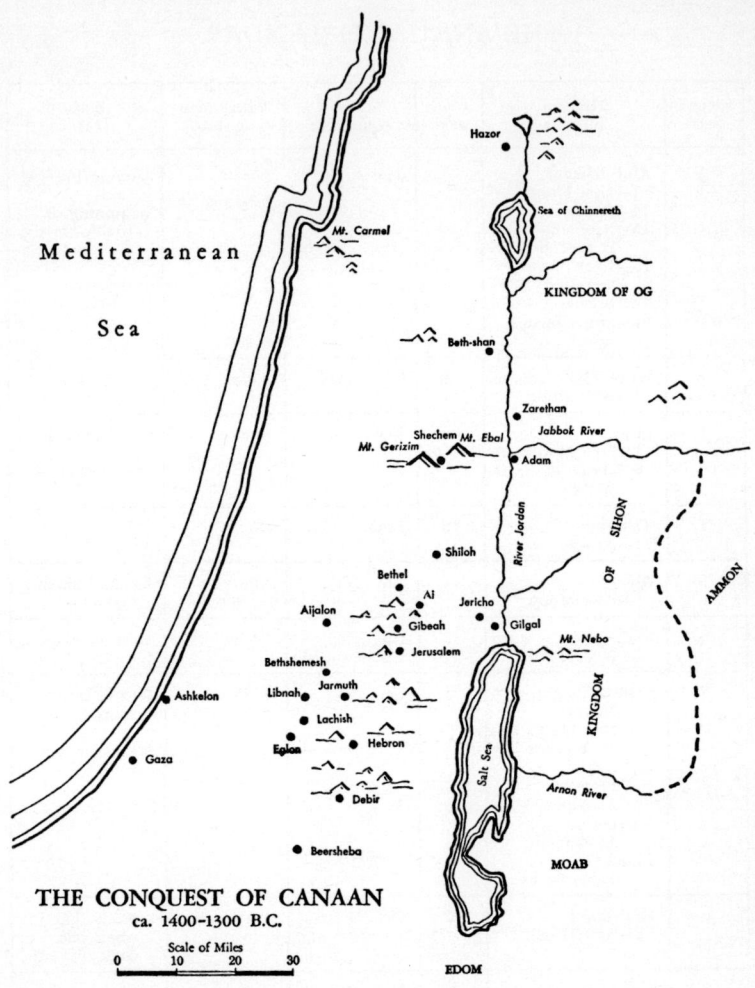

Figure 4

APPENDIX / 181

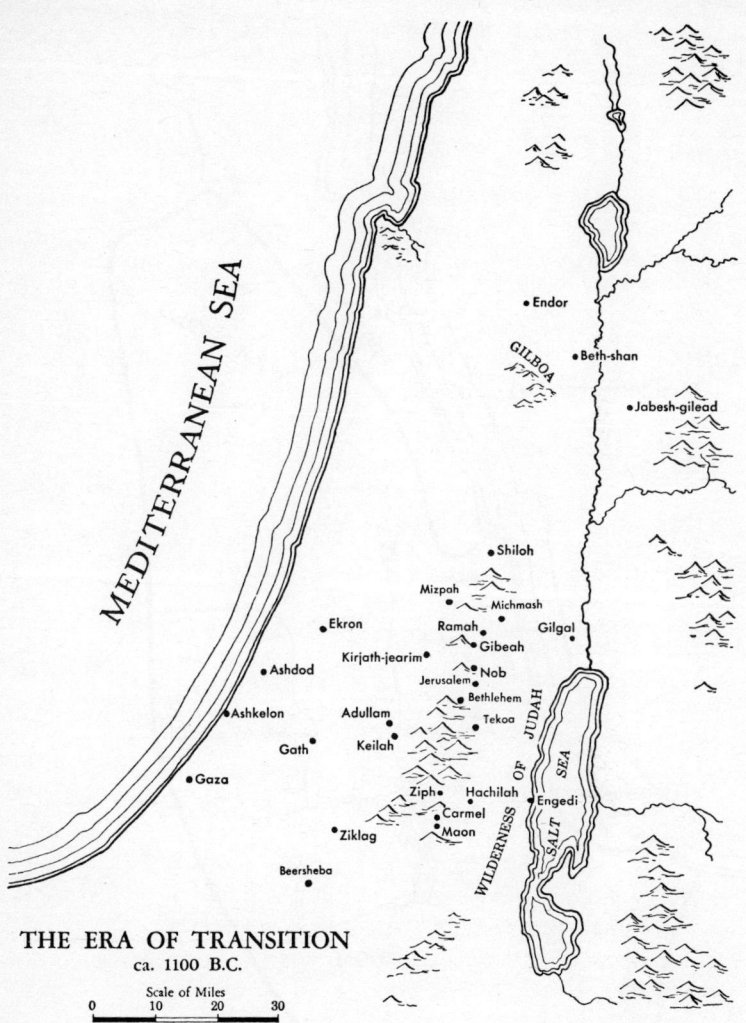

Figure 5

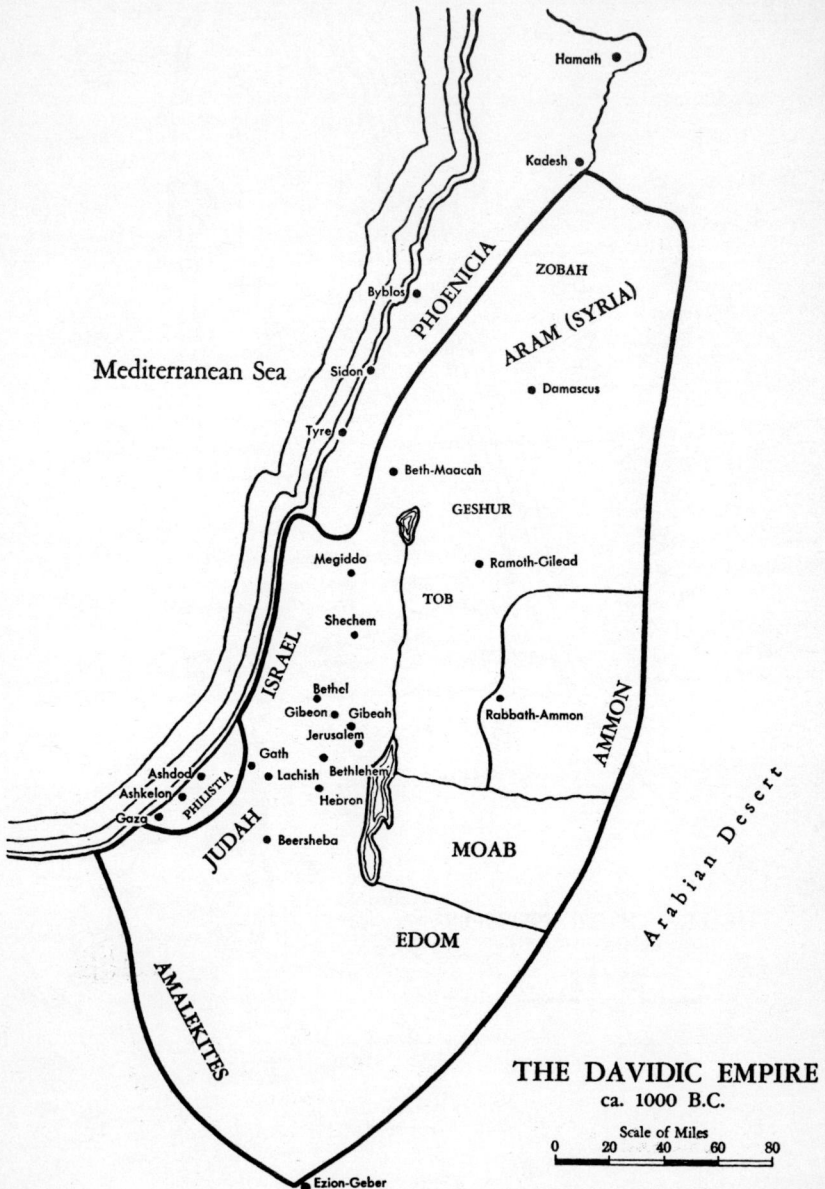

Figure 6

APPENDIX / 183

KINGS AND PROPHETS—DIVIDED KINGDOM, 931-586

Date	Northern K.	Prophets	Southern K.	Assyria	Syria
931	*Jeroboam Dyn.* Jeroboam	Ahijah Shemaiah Iddo	Rehoboam Abijah		Rezon
909	Nadab *Baasha Dyn.* Baasha	Azariah Hanani Jehu	Asa		
885	Elah (Zimri) *Omri Dynasty* Omri (Tibni) Ahab	Elijah Micaiah Eliezer	Jehoshaphat	Ashurnasirpal	Benhadad
841	Ahaziah Joram *Jehu Dynasty* Jehu	Elisha Jehoiada Zechariah	Jehoram Ahaziah Athaliah Joash	Shalmaneser III	Hazael
	Jehoahaz Jehoash Jeroboam II	Jonah Hosea Amos	Amaziah Azariah		Benhadad
752	Zechariah *Last Kings* Shallum Menahem Pekahiah Pekah Hoshea	Isaiah Oded	Jotham Ahaz	Tiglath-pileser III Shalmaneser V Sargon II	Rezin
722	*Fall of Samaria*	Micah	Hezekiah Manasseh	Sennacherib Esarhaddon Ashurbanipal	
640		Jeremiah Huldah	Amon Josiah Jehoahaz Jehoiakim Jehoiachin	*Babylon* Nabopolassar Nebuchadnezzar	
586		(Ezekiel) (Daniel)	Zedekiah *Fall of Jerusalem*		

Figure 7

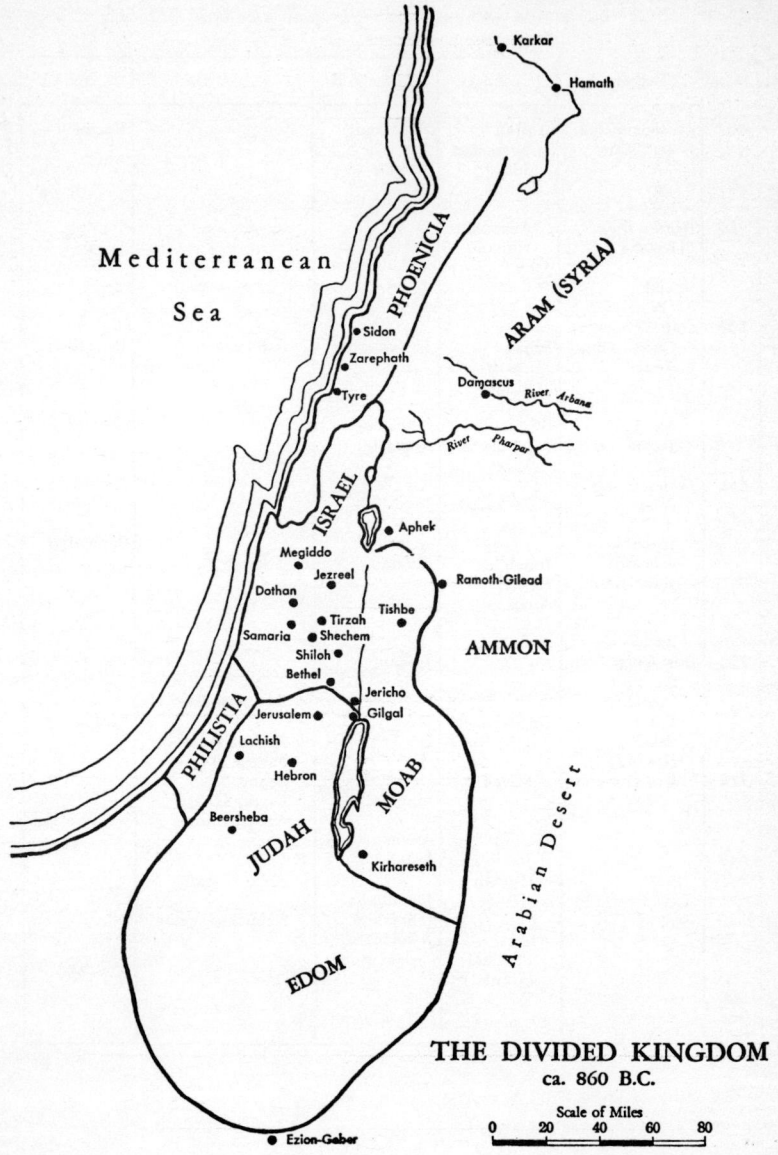

Figure 8

APPENDIX / 185

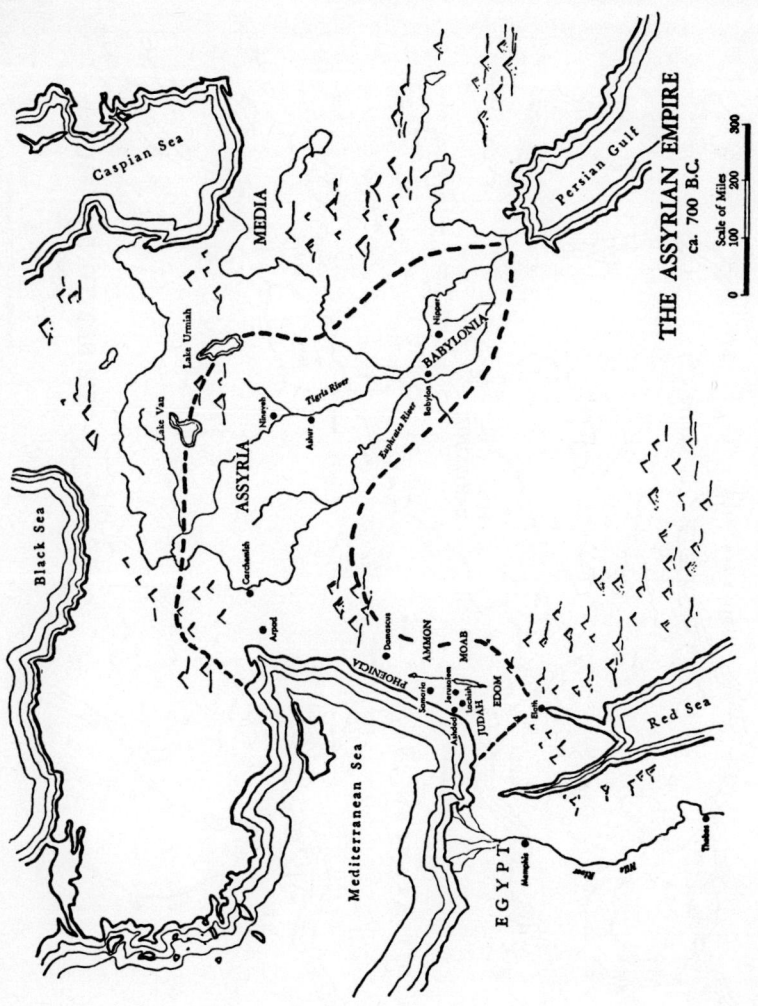

Figure 9

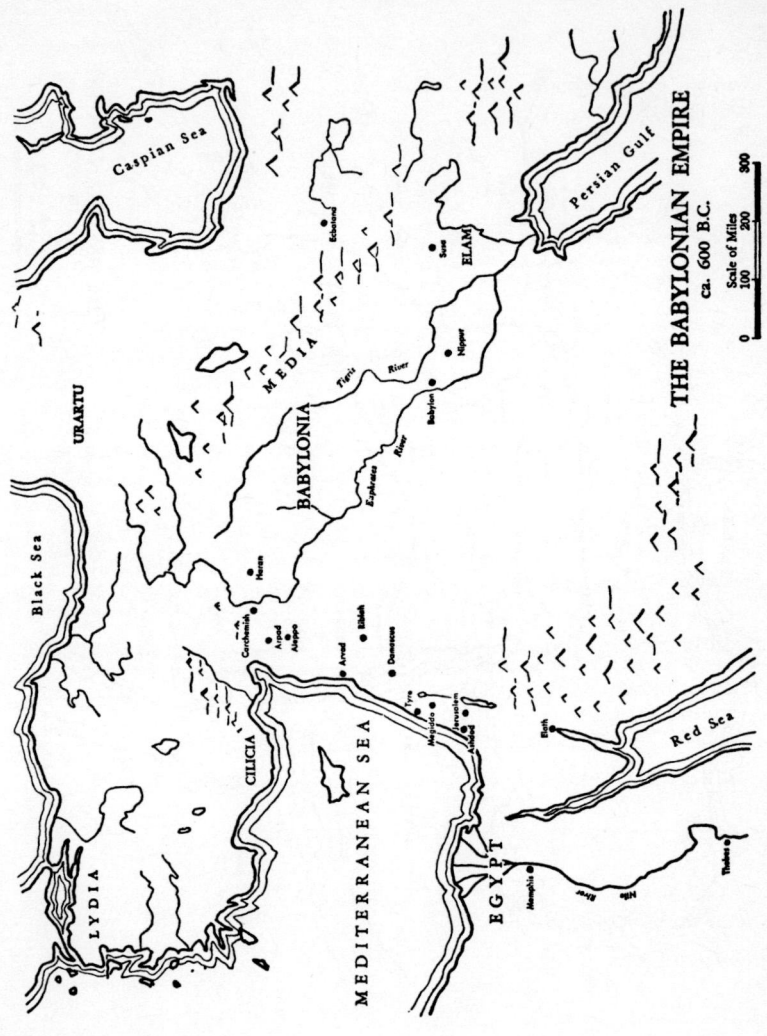

Figure 10

APPENDIX / 187

Exilic Times

	JUDAH	BABYLON	MEDO-PERSIA	EGYPT
639	Josiah			
626		Nabopolassar		
609	Jehoahaz Jehoiakim			Necho
605		Nebuchadnezzar		
597	Jehoiachin Zedekiah			Psammetichus
594				
588				Apries
586	Jerusalem destroyed			
568				Amasis
562		Awel-Marduk		
560		Neriglissar		
559			Cyrus	
556		Nabonidus (Belshazzar)		
539	Edict— return of the Jews	Fall of Babylon		
530			Cambyses	
522	Zerubbabel Haggai, Zechariah		Darius	
515	Temple completed			
485			Xerxes	
479			(Esther)	
464			Artaxerxes I	
457	Ezra			
444	Nehemiah			
423			Darius II	
404			Artaxerxes II	

Figure 11

SCRIPTURE INDEX

OLD TESTAMENT

Genesis 1:1–11:32, 5–9; 3:15, 57; 12:1–50:26, 10–19; 15:16, 40; 17:1–27, 41; 36:12, 48; 41:52, 66; 44:7, 65
Exodus 1:1–18:27, 20–27; 17:8–16, 40; 19:6, 61; 19:1–40:38, 28–30; 29:38, 112; 40:34, 62
Leviticus 1:1–27:34, 30–32; 9:23–24, 62; 18:24–28, 40; 23:34–35, 112; 25:42, 55, 61
Numbers 1:1–36:13, 32–34; 13:1–14:45, 40
Deuteronomy 1:1–34:12, 34–35; 7:1–6, 40; 12:31, 40; 17:14–20, 51, 62; 17:17, 59, 63
Joshua 1:1–24:33, 36–43 24:2, 16
Judges 1:1–21:35, 44–46
Ruth 1:1–4:22, 46
1 Samuel 1:1–31:13, 47–54
2 Samuel 1:1–24:25, 54–60
1 Kings 1:1–11:43, 61–64; 3:3–28, 133; 4:29–30, 133; 5:12, 133; 6:1, 24; 12:1–22:58, 65 ff.; 14:25–26, 47; 18:19, 39
2 Kings 1:1–25:30, 65–106; 21:7, 39; 25:27–30, 109
1 Chronicles 1:1–29:30, 54–60
2 Chronicles 1:1–9:31, 61–64; 8:14, 123; 9:1–24, 133; 10:1–36:23, 65–106; 35:25, 155
Ezra 1:1–6:22, 111–116; 1:1–2:70, 112; 4:8–6:18, 2; 5:1–6:22, 114; 7:1–10:44, 118–119

Nehemiah 1:1–13:31, 120–124
Esther 1:1–10:3, 116–118
Job 1:1–42:17, 125–130
Psalms 1:1–150:6, 130–132; 18, 58; 32, 59; 51, 59; 103:17–18, 40
Proverbs 1:1–31:31, 132–134
Ecclesiastes 1:1–12:14, 134–136
Song of Songs 1:1–8:14, 136–138
Isaiah 1:1–66:24, 139–153; 36–39, 97–99; 41:8, 16; 45:1–4, 112; 50:1, 137; 54:4–5, 137; 66:1–24, 40
Jeremiah 1:1–52:34, 154–157; 3:1–20, 138; 9:23–24, 40; 10:11, 2; 25:11–12, 105; 26, 158; 28, 159; 29, 159; 29:10, 105; 39:3,13, 109; 52:31–34 109
Lamentations 1:1–5:22, 157; 3:22, 40
Ezekiel 1:1–48:35, 157–161; 1:1, 109; 16, 138; 23, 138; 29:17, 109
Daniel 1:1–12:13, 161–164; 1:1, 105; 1:17–21, 108; 2:1–49, 108; 2:4–7:28, 2; 4:30, 108; 5:1–30, 111; 6:1–28, 111; 7:25, 111; 8:27, 111; 9:1–27, 111; 10:1–12:13, 111
Hosea 1:1–14:9, 165–167; 1–3, 138
Joel 1:1–3:21, 167
Amos 1:1–9:15, 165–166
Obadiah 1–21, 169
Jonah 1:1–4:11, 165–166
Micah 1:1–7:20, 167–168
Nahum 1:1–3:19, 169–170
Habakkuk 1:1–3:19, 169–170
Zephaniah 1:1–3:20, 167–168
Haggai 1:1–2:23, 170; 1:1–15, 114

Zechariah 1:1–14:21, 171–172; 1:1, 114
Malachi 1:1–4:6, 172–173

NEW TESTAMENT

Matthew 1:1; 56; 11:10, 14, 173; 22:29, 43–45, 4; 22:34–40, 34
Mark 12:28–32, 34
Luke 10:25–28, 34; 16:17, 4; 24:25, 4
John 10:34–35, 4
Acts 7:22, 34
2 Corinthians 1:3, 40
2 Timothy 3:16, 4
Hebrews 11:32, 45, 46
2 Peter 1:20–21, 4
James 2:23, 16

SUBJECT INDEX

Aaron, 30, 33, 50, 118
Abdon, 46
Abel, 7, 8
Abiathar, 53
Abijah, 76, 88
Abimelech: priest, 52, 53; son of Gideon, 45
Abinadab, 50, 56
Abiram, 33
Abraham (Abram), 6, 9, 10–16, 28, 34
Absalom, 60
Achan, 41
Achish, 52, 53
Adadnirari III, 70, 71
Adam, 6, 7, 67
Adonis-Tammuz, 137
Adullam, 52
Agur, 134
Ahab: false prophet, 159; king of Israel, 69, 71, 76, 78–81, 89, 90, 100
Ahasuerus. See Xerxes
Ahaz, 70, 72, 85, 96, 97, 140, 143, 147
Ahaziah: son of Ahab, 66, 79; son of Jehoram 80, 91
Ahijah, 63, 64, 75
Ahikam, 104, 156
Ai, 42
Akh-en-Aton (Amen-hotep IV), 21, 23
Akitu, 162
Akkad, 10, 14
Aleppo, 14
Alexander the Great, 10, 21, 113
Amalekites, 32, 33, 40, 45, 52, 55, 58
Amarna, 21, 37

Amaziah, 82, 92, 93, 94, 139
Amen-em-ope, Wisdom of, 133
Amen-hotep II, 37
Ammonites, 45, 48, 51, 58, 59, 82, 96, 100
Amnon, 60
Amon, 101
Amorites, 11, 33, 38, 43
Amos, 83, 84, 140, 166, 168
Amos, Book of, 166
Amun cult, 21, 22
Anath, 39
Anathoth, 103, 154, 155
Apadana, 118
Aphek, 79
Agabah, 54, 62, 94, 139
Arabah, 62
Arabs, 120, 121
Aram (Syria), 48, 58, 59, 64, 65ff.
Araxes (River), 62
Aristotle, 135
Armenia, 114
Arnon (River), 33, 43
Artabanus, 118
Artatama, 37
Artaxerxes I (Longimanus), 116, 118, 120
Aryans, 37, 38
Asa, 68, 76, 88
Asaph, 98, 130
Asenath, 18
Ashburdan III, 72
Ashdod, 47, 73, 121, 141, 147
Asherah, 39, 78, 100
Ashkelon, 47

Ashtoreth (Astarte) 39, 63
Ashur: Assyrian god, 70; city of, 73, 102, 103
Ashurbanipal, 73, 74, 101, 102, 107, 157, 158, 169
Ashurnasirpal II, 69, 71
Ashurnirari, 72
Assyria, 37, 66, 70–74ff.
Astarte (Ashtoreth), 63
Athaliah, 77, 89, 90, 91, 167
Athens, 118
Aton, 21
Atonement, 150, 151
Atonement, Day of, 31, 122
Avaris (Zoan), 12, 36
Awel-marduk (Evil Merodach), 109
Azariah: Abednego, 161; king. See Uzziah
Azekah, 42

Baal, 39, 44, 78, 80, 91, 100, 103
Baasha, 68, 76, 80, 88
Babel, Tower of, 9
Babylon, 11, 36, 38, 154ff.
Balaam, 33
Balak, 33
Barak, 45
Baruch, 156
Bashan, 81
Bathsheba, 59
Beeroth, 42
Beersheba, 13, 14, 32, 50, 141
Bel, 113
Bel-ibni, 98, 142
Belshazzar, 110, 111, 161, 163
Benhadad, 68–71, 76, 78, 80, 82, 83, 88
Benjamin, 45, 51, 65, 66
Bethel, 14, 17, 42, 75, 76, 81, 103
Beth-horon, 42
Bethlehem, 50, 166, 168
Bildad, 127–130
Black Obelisk, 21, 81
Boghazköy, 37, 38
Borsippa, 108
Byblos, 47

Cain, 7, 8
Calah, 71, 73
Caleb, 32, 34
Cambyses, 112, 113

Canaan: geography of, 10–13; religion of, 39, 40, 50
Canaanites (Phoenecians), 48
Carchemish, 38, 48, 74, 105, 107
Carmel (Mount), 78, 113
Chaldean, 127, 170
Chronicles: First book of, 54–60; Second book of, 61–106
Croesus, 110
Cyrus, 110–113, 149, 150, 164

Damascus, 48, 58, 64, 68–70, 72, 78, 80, 83–85, 92, 96, 107, 141, 144, 165
Dan, 13, 46, 50, 75, 81, 141
Daniel (Belteshazzar), 105, 107–111, 158, 160
Daniel, Book of, 161–164
Danube, 115
Darius, The Mede, 111, 161, 163
Darius I, 113, 114–116, 172
Dathan, 33
David, 48, 52–60, 65–67, 70, 71, 77, 83, 91–94, 96, 98, 100, 102, 107, 108, 112, 114, 123, 130–132, 134, 140, 143–147, 154, 161
Day of Atonement, 31, 122
Dead Sea, 43, 83, 165
Dead Sea Scrolls, 143
Debir (Kirjath-sepher), 43
Deborah, 45, 46
Decalogue, 28–35, 63, 86
Deuteronomy, Book of, 34–35
Dothan, 17
Dura, 162

Ebal (Mount), 40, 42
Ebed-melech, 155
Ebla (Tell Mardikh), 14
Ecbatana, 110, 114, 115, 116
Ecclesiastes, Book of, 134–136
Edom, 33, 48, 58, 64, 70, 79, 90, 93, 101, 147, 161, 169
Edomites, 82, 85
Egypt, religion of, 22–23
Ehud, 45
Ekron, 47, 98
El, 39, 47
Elah, 76
Elam, 11, 116

SUBJECT INDEX / 193

Elath, 33, 62, 85, 94, 139
Eleazar, 43
Eli, 49, 50
Eliakim. *See* Jehoiakim
Eliashib, 124
Eliezer: prophet, 90; servant of Abraham, 14
Elihu, 129
Elijah, 39, 78, 79, 80, 172
Eliphaz, 127-130
Elisha, 78-82
Elkosh, 169
Elon, 46
Eltekah, 98
Endor, woman of, 53
Ephraim: northern kingdom, 66, 172; tribe, 82, 87
Epicurean, 136
Esagila Temple of Marduk, 109, 116
Esarhaddon, 73, 100, 101
Esau, 16, 48, 168, 169
Esdraelon, 77
Esther, 116
Esther, Book of, 116-117
Ethan, 130
Ethbaal, 69, 77
Eve, 6, 7
Evil Merodach. *See* Awel-marduk
Ezekiel, 105, 109, 138, 157-161
Ezekiel, Book of, 109, 143, 157-161
Ezida Temple, 109, 110
Ezion-geber, 62, 90
Ezra, 118, 119, 122, 123, 131, 149
Ezra, Book of, 1-6, 114-115; 7-10, 118-119

Feast of Trumpets, 122
Feast of Weeks, 31-32
Feasts of Tabernacles, 32, 61, 112, 122, 135
Fertile Crescent, 10ff.

Gad: prophet, 51, 52; tribe, 34
Galilee, 13, 76
Gath, 47, 52, 70, 80
Gath Hepher, 165
Gaumata, 113
Gaza, 13, 43, 47
Genesis, The Book of, 5-19, 143
Gerar, 14

Gerizim (Mount), 40
Geshem, 120
Geshur, 48, 60
Gezer, 43
Gibeah, 52, 55, 56
Gibeon, 42, 43, 61
Gideon, 45, 46
Gihon, 98
Gilboa (Mount), 53, 55
Gilead, 45, 78, 79, 81
Gilgal, 41, 43, 50, 52
Giza, 12
Gobryas, 110
Gog, 161
Goliath, 52, 54
Gomorrah, 14, 16
Goshen, 19, 21
Greeks, 63, 108, 163, 165
Guti, 11

Habakkuk, The Book of, 170
Hadad: an Edomite, 64; a god, 39
Hedadazer, 68
Hagar, 15
Haggai, 114, 171
Haggai, The Book of, 114, 170
Haman, 117
Hamath, 48, 54, 68-70, 79, 83, 165
Hammurabi, Code of, 11, 15, 36
Hanani: a prophet, 89; Shadrach, 161
Hananiah, 155, 158
Haran, 14, 37, 74, 107, 110
Harris, R. Laird, 1
Hattusil, 38
Hazael, 69-73, 78, 80-83, 92, 165
Hazor (Tell el-Qedah), 43
Hebron, 14, 17, 42, 43, 55-57, 60
Hegel, 135
Heliopolis (On) 22
Heman, 130
Heshbon, 33
Heri-Hor, 47
Hermon, 43
Hezekiah, 67, 97-99, 101, 134, 141, 142, 145, 147, 148, 149, 168
Hilkiah, 102
Hinnom, 100
Hiram, 48, 61
Hittites, 16, 22, 37, 38, 59
Hivites, 37

Hophni, 49
Hor, 33
Horeb, 78, 80. See also Sinai
Horus, 22
Hosea, 83, 84, 138, 140
Hosea, Book of, 166–167
Hoshea, 70, 72, 86, 97, 141
Huldah, 102, 103
Hurrians (Horites), 37
Hyksos, 12, 21, 24, 36

Ibzan, 46
Ichabod, 50
Imhotep, 12
Immanuel, 144
Isaac, 16, 28, 34
Isaiah: Book of, 139–153; person, 96, 100, 112, 137
Ishmael, 18
Ishtar: Gate of, 108; goddess, 63
Israel: Jacob and, 17; Northern Kingdom of, 65ff.; nation of, 20ff.; religion of, 28–35

Jabesh (Jabesh-gilead) 51
Jabin, 45
Jacob, 16–19, 28, 34
Jair, 45
Jarmuth, 42
Jaxartes, 111
Jebusites, 55
Jeconiah. See Jehoiachin
Jehoahaz: son of Jehu, 62, 89; son of Josiah (Shallum) 104, 155, 158
Jehoash (King of Israel), 70, 82, 93. See also Joash
Jehoiachin (Jeconiah), 105, 108, 112, 155, 162
Jehoiada, 91, 92, 167
Jehoikim (Eliakim), 103, 104, 107, 155, 156, 158
Jehoram, King of Judah, 77, 89, 90. See also Joram
Jehoshaphat, 67, 77, 79, 89, 90
Jehosheba, 91
Jehu: dynasty of, 81–83; king, 66, 67, 69, 71, 75; prophet, 76
Jephthah, 45
Jeremiah, 104, 105, 137, 143, 154, 158; Book of, 154–157

Jericho, 41, 77
Jeroboam I: dynasty of, 75–76; king, 64, 65, 67, 75–76, 80, 82, 87
Jeroboam II, 70, 82–83, 93, 95, 103, 139, 165, 166
Jesus Christ, 3, 56, 132, 138
Jethro (Reuel), 25
Jezebel, 39, 69, 77–80, 90, 91, 101
Jezreel, 53, 80, 91
Joab, 59, 60
Joash, King of Judah, 91, 92, 167. See also Jehoash
Job, Book of, 125–130, 160
Joel, Book of, 167
Jonah, 83; Book of, 165–166
Jonathan, 52, 55
Joppa, 73, 98
Joram, King of Israel, 66, 69, 79, 80, 90. See also Jehoram
Jordan River, 13
Joseph, 10, 17–19, 24, 65
Josephus, 109
Joshua: the priest, 114, 171, 172; son of Nun, 32, 34, 36–43, 122
Joshua, Book of, 36–43
Josiah, 63, 67, 101–104, 154, 155, 157, 158, 168
Jotham, 72, 85, 95, 96, 139, 147
Judah: nation of, (Southern Kingdom) 65ff.; tribe of, 55, 65, 66
Judges, Book of, 44–46

Kadesh on the Orontes, 37, 38
Kadesh or Kadesh-barnea, 32, 43
Kant, 135
Karkar, the Battle of, 66, 69, 71, 79, 89
Karnak, 21, 23, 47
Kebar River, 159
Kephirah, 42
Khorsabad, 73
Kings: First Book of, 61–64, 65ff.; Second Book of, 65–106
Kiriath, 42
Kirjath Jearim, 50, 56
Korah, 33, 130

Laban, 16, 17
Labashi-Marduk, 110
Lachish (Tell ed-Duweir), 42, 43, 93

SUBJECT INDEX / 195

Lamentations, Book of, 157
Layard, 81
Leah, 16
Lebanon, 43
Lemuel, 134
Leviticus, Book of, 30-32
Libnah, 43, 99
Lot, 14, 16
Luxor, 23
Lydia, 110

Maacah, 48, 88
Makkedah, 42, 43
Malachi, 172
Manasseh: king, 39, 100, 101, 103, 142, 149, 169; tribe of, 34
Mardikh. See Ebla
Marduk, 11, 110-113, 116
Mari, 11
Mattan, 91
Mattaniah (Zedekiah), 105
Media, 36, 74, 114, 157, 163, 164, 166, 169
Megiddo, 37, 44, 80, 86, 91
Megilloth, 135
Memphis, 12, 21
Menahem, 72, 84, 95, 140
Menes, 11, 22
Merodach-baladan, 98, 142, 149
Merom, 43
Mesopotamia, 10, 14, 15, 17, 19, 24, 44
Messiah, 57, 132, 143
Micah (Idolator), 46
Micah, Book of, 167-168
Micaiah, 79
Michael, 164
Michal, 59
Michmash, 52
Midianites, 18, 25, 45
Milcom, 63
Miletus, 111
Mishael (Meshach), 161
Mitanni, 36, 37
Mizpah, 50, 51
Moab, 33, 35, 45, 58, 77, 90, 101, 147
Moabites, 48, 79
Moabite Stone, 77
Molech, 63, 100
Mordecai, 116, 117
Moriah, 60

Moses, 24-35, 62, 75, 88, 112, 114, 118, 122, 130, 141
Mycale, Cape, battle of 116

Naaman, 80
Nabonassar, 66
Nabonidus, 110, 111
Nabopolassar, 107
Naboth, 79, 80
Nabu, 162
Nadab, 76
Nahum, Book of, 169-170
Nal, 96, 140
Nannar, 11, 14
Napoleon, 21
Naram-sin, 11, 14
Nathan, 50, 56, 57, 59
Nazareth, 165
Nebo, Mount, 35
Nebo, a god, 109, 110, 113
Nebuchadnezzar, 105, 107, 108, 116, 150, 161-163
Necho II (Pharaoh), 104
Negeb, 14
Nehemiah, 120, 149, 172
Nehemiah, Book of, 120-124
Nineveh, 73, 74, 83, 102, 107, 158, 166, 169, 170
Nin-Gal, 11
Noah, 8, 9, 160
Nob, 52
Northern Kingdom, 65 ff. See also Israel
Numbers, Book of, 32-34
Nuzi Tablets, 13, 15, 16

Obadiah, Book of, 169
Obed-edom, 56
Oded, 85
Offerings: burnt, 31; grain, 31; peace (fellowship) 31; sin, (purification) 31; guilt (trespass) 31
Og, 33
Omri, 67, 69, 76, 77, 83
Omride Dynasty, 76-79
On (Heliopolis), 18
Orontes River, 37, 68, 69
Osiris, 23
Othniel, 45, 46
Oxus, 111

196 / SUBJECT INDEX

Padi, 98
Pasargadae, 113
Passover, The, 20, 27, 31, 41, 98, 102, 114, 115, 137, 141, 157
Pekah, 70, 72, 84–86, 96, 140, 141, 144
Pekahiah, 84, 140
Pelusium, 113
Persepolis, 115, 117
Philistines, 54ff.
Phinehas, 49
Phoenicians, 2, 21, 48, 54, 56, 61–63, 69ff.
Plataea, Battle of, 116
Potiphar, 18, 19
Proverbs, Book of, 132–134
Psalms, Book of, 130–132, 143
Ptah-hotep, 12
Ptolemy, 66
Purim, 117

Rabbath (Rabbath Ammon), 59
Rachel, 16, 17
Rahab, 41
Ramah, 50, 68, 76, 88
Ramses II, 22, 37, 38
Ramses III, 38, 47
Ramoth-gilead, 80, 89
Ras Shamra. *See* Ugarit
Re, 22
Rebekah, 16
Red Sea, The 64, 94, 115
Rehoboam, 47, 67, 68, 75, 87–88
Religion: of Canaanites, 39–40; of Egypt, 22–23; of Israel, 28–35
Revel. *See* Jethro
Rezin, 70, 72, 84–85, 96, 140, 143
Rezon, 64, 68
Riblah, 104
Russia, 115
Ruth, 46; Book of, 46

Sabbath, 31, 123, 124
Sabeans, 127
Saduris III, 95
Salamis, Battle of, 116
Samaria, 65, 67, 70, 71, 76ff.
Samson, 46, 47
Samuel, 47–54

Samuel: First Book of, 47–54; Second Book of, 54–60
Sanballat, 120, 124
Sarah, 15
Sardis, 110, 111, 115
Sargon II, 73, 86, 97, 98, 141
Saul, 47, 51–55, 59, 65
Scythians, 115
Seir, 93
Sennacherib, 73, 98, 99, 100, 134, 142
Seth, 8
Shabako, 98, 141
Shakespeare, 126
Shallum: king of Israel, 83, 84; king of Judah. *See* Jehoahaz
Shalmaneser III, 66, 69, 71, 79, 81
Shalmaneser IV, 72
Shalmaneser V, 72, 73, 86
Shamgar, 45
Shamshi-Adad I, 11
Shamshi-Adad V, 72
Shamash-shum-ukin, 73, 101
Sheba, Benjamite, 60; Queen of, 62, 133
Shechem, 14, 17, 40, 65, 75, 77
Shemaiah: a captive, 159; a prophet, 87
Sheshbazzar, 112
Shiloh, 43, 49
Shinar, 9
Shishak, 87
Shulammite, 137, 138
Sidon, 48, 69, 73, 77, 98
Sihon, 33
Siloam Tunnel, 98, 142
Sin, moon-god, 110
Sinai (Horeb), 14, 27, 28, 31, 32, 61
Sinuhe, 12
Sippor, 110, 113
Sisera, 45
Sodom, 14, 16
Solomon, 56, 57, 60–64, 70, 71, 75, 77, 83, 95, 106, 114, 123, 130–138, 140, 158
Song of Songs, 136–138
Southern Kingdom (Judah), 65ff.
Sphinx, 135
Sumerians, 10, 11
Susa (Shushan), 11, 109, 110, 115, 116, 118, 120
Syria (Aram), 14, 24, 36, 37, 38, 65ff.

Taanach, 44
Taharka (Tirhakah), 73
Tanis, 47
Tattenai, 114
Taurus, 109
Tekoah, 166
Tell-el-Hesi, 43, 43
Tema, 110
Terah, 9
Thebes, 12, 21, 23, 47, 71, 73, 101, 169
Thermopylae, Battle of, 116
Thiele, E. R. 66
Thrace, 115
Thutmose III, 21, 37
Thutmose IV, 37
Tiglath-pileser I, 71
Tiglath-pileser III (Pul), 70, 72, 84, 95, 97, 102, 111, 139, 140, 141, 147, 167
Tirhakah (Taharka), 99
Tirzah, 65, 76
Tob, 48
Tobiah, 120
Toi, 68
Tola, 45
Torah, 118
Tut-ankh-Amon, 21, 22
Tyre, 48, 61, 82

Ugarit (Ras Shamra), 38
Ur, 10, 11, 14
Urartu, 84, 95, 96, 140
Uriah: the Hittite, 59; the Prophet, 158

Urijah, 59
Urim, 53
Ur-nammu, 11
Uz, 126
Uzziah (Azariah), 67, 72, 84, 92, 93–96, 97, 139, 140, 168

Vashti, 116

Washshukanni, 37
Wellhausen, J., 13
Wen-Amun, 47

Xerxes (Ahasuerus), 116

Zechariah: Book of, 114, 170–171; king of Israel, 83; post-exilic prophet, 114; prophet in Southern Kingdom, 92, 95, 140
Zedekiah: false prophet, 159; king of Judah, (Mattaniah), 105, 155, 156, 162
Zephaniah: Book of, 168; the prophet, 168
Zerubbabel, 112, 114, 149, 171
Ziklag, 48, 53, 56
Zimri, 76
Zimri-lim, 11
Zion, 131, 143–146, 148, 150–153, 168, 169
Zipporah, 25
Zobah, 48, 68
Zophar, 127–130